Endorsements for *7 Secrets of Worry-Free Living*

"Back to the Bible has conducted extensive research, which has been thoroughly incorporated into these pages. I love how *Worry-Free Living* engages me with such relevant facts, but what I really appreciate is that Arnie and Michael have developed a tool that can assist us all in our dialogue with one another. The 'Recap and Reflect' feature helps me to hear from God through others—and that may be the most important thing of all."

—Brian Doyle
President, Iron Sharpens Iron National Men's Equipping Conferences
www.ironsharpensiron.net

"Great advice for *every* worrier in your life—from an anxious child to a stressed-out spouse. The authors guide readers toward a clear understanding of worry and anxiety, and they offer hands-on strategies for relief. Explore *Worry-Free Living* on your own or with a group and learn how to nurture a calmer, Christ-centered home front."

—Dr. Trina Young Greer
Licensed Clinical Psychologist,
Founder and Executive Director of Genesis Counseling Center
www.genesiscounselingcenter.com

"In *Worry-Free Living*, Arnie and Michael give you the practical tools and common-sense strategies that can help break the grip of unproductive worry, anxiety, and stress in your life. Like personal trainers, they use biblical principles, stories, and research findings to give you effective tools to live in peace and freedom through the healing power of Jesus Christ. More than another 'self-help' book, *Worry-Free Living* is a developmental spiritual fitness plan for individuals or small groups who are seeking to live more effectively for Christ and His Kingdom."

—Dr. Rick Ryding
Pastor and Professor Emeritus (Mount Vernon, Ohio)

"God is not just interested in our souls; He wraps his salvation around the *whole* person. This is why the mind, body, spirit approach to handling worry is essential for wholeness and healing. *Worry-Free Living* is a biblically grounded book that provides helpful, practical tools for families. And the couple and group discussion worksheets, paired with the Bible studies, make this a valuable resource for churches."

—Rev. Connie Larson DeVaughn
Co-Pastor, Altadena Baptist Church
www.altadenabaptist.org

"We wholeheartedly recommend *Worry-Free Living* for every family and church leader. Page after page is grounded in Scripture and filled with thought-provoking questions, making this a useful resource for group study. *Worry-Free Living* is outstanding, excellent in truth, very well written, and highly practical."

— Dr. Steve and Megan Scheibner
Founders of CharacterHealth, Creators of the YouTube video
"In My Seat: A Pilot's Story" www.CharacterHealth.com

SEVEN 7 SECRETS

OF **WORRY-FREE LIVING**

FINDING
FREEDOM
FROM
FEAR, ANXIETY
& STRESS

Arnie Cole & Michael Ross

BroadStreet
PUBLISHING

Published by BroadStreet Publishing, LLC
Racine, Wisconsin, USA
www.broadstreetpublishing.com

SEVEN SECRETS OF WORRY-FREE LIVING
FINDING FREEDOM FROM FEAR, ANXIETY, AND STRESS

ISBN: 978-1-4245-5063-0 (hard cover)
ISBN: 978-1-4245-5064-7 (e-book)

Content for this book was revised by Michael Ross from
Worry-Free Living by Dr. Arnie Cole & Michael Ross
Licensed from Authentic Publishers
188 Front Street, Suite 116-44
Franklin, TN 37064
Authentic Publishers is a division of Authentic Media, Inc.

Cover design by Chris Garborg at www.garborgdesign.com
Interior design and typesetting by Katherine Lloyd at www.theDESKonline.com

Printed in China

15 16 17 18 19 20   7 6 5 4 3 2 1

CONTENTS

WHEN WORRY HITS HOME

It's a boisterous, kid-centric weekend in the Meyer household, and thirty-nine-year-old Marci wouldn't have it any other way. While other moms would give anything for a bit of quiet—*an hour at the spa would be heaven, right?*—she savors the noise.

The squeals and giggles of her three children are music to her ears, a reminder of what's most important: her family's well-being.

Life itself.

The young Florida mom shudders as she thinks back over the past six months: the fear, the worry, the stress … all the what-ifs that have incessantly plagued her and her husband's thoughts. It's the possibility of losing what's so precious to them.

From across the family room, Marci watches eight-year-old Andrew, her middle child, sprawled on the floor, lost in a world of play. She can't take her eyes off of him.

Andrew meticulously snaps Legos into place as he carefully inspects his creation. "Here's the command center," he tells a playmate. "And these lasers blast enemy destroyers."

"That's so cool," his buddy says as he skillfully lands a ship behind Lego walls. "The good guys can hide their cruisers around the arena."

A mishmash of white, red, and yellow bricks rise into an eclectic fortress—complete with medieval towers, battlements, and working catapults. On the other side of the wall are futuristic spaceships and what looks like a giant stadium. Is it an interplanetary outpost? An academy for brave cadets with a *Hunger Games* twist?

"Time for the Beyblade battle!" shouts another friend.

Andrew's eyes light up. "Let it rip!" he shouts, in the words of his favorite game.

The kids scramble to claim the coolest spin-top toys: brightly colored discs with names like "Guardian Leviathan," "Pirate Orochi," and "Ninja Salamander." Seconds later they pull plastic rip cords and launch their Beyblades into the makeshift arena.

Soon they're immersed in an imaginary world of adventurous and courageous warriors, fighting for justice against evil dystopian kingdoms in far-off galaxies.

Marci smiles at all the commotion.

Just how it should be, she thinks. *Kids lost in play. Not how it's been lately. Day after day after day full of stress and anxiety, with challenges no child should face.*

She quietly watches Andrew interacting, savoring his expressions, making mental audio files of his laughter and snapshots of the joy that always seems to radiate from his precious face.

With the exception of his shiny bald head, nobody would think the boy had a care in the world. No one would suspect he's ill.

Terribly ill.

A real-life war is being waged within the Meyer home. Andrew is battling a mostly invisible monster—a growth of abnormal cells in his body that threatens his young life.

I wonder if he gets it, Marci thinks. *I wonder how much he understands what's going on. Maybe it's okay if he doesn't. Maybe it's okay if I do all his worrying for him.*

A few months earlier, Andrew was diagnosed with non-Hodgkin's lymphoma—a cancer that affects the lymphatic network, part of the circulatory system. The lymph nodes or glands are positioned all around the body, and one of their main responsibilities is fighting infections.

The trouble all started in August 2012.

※

Marci and her husband, Jeff, had noticed that Andrew was suddenly talking differently—much as if he'd developed a slight speech impediment or maybe had just returned from a trip to the orthodontist. The concerned mom examined his tongue. "Nothing strange here," she said. Then she squinted and ran a fingernail over a tooth. "That is—nothing a toothbrush and a good cleaning can't fix!"

Andrew laughed.

The boy had no past health issues and rarely got sick. And, at that moment, he wasn't complaining of, for instance, a painful tongue or a sore throat. But a few weeks later—on September 19, to be exact—his condition began to worsen.

"It hurts a little," he told his parents, "like when I eat or swallow."

Marci put her hand on his forehead. "You don't feel hot, but if your throat hurts it's possible you caught a bug, maybe strep. We'll go see the family doctor."

Later that day Andrew sat on an exam table with his mouth opened wide. Their concerned physician was nodding her head and scribbling notes on a pad. "Makes complete sense that he's having a hard time talking," she said, finally turning toward Marci. "He has a 'golf ball' in the back of his throat. Take a look."

Marci bent to inspect, followed the light, and gasped. "That's *huge*. Exactly what is it?"

"An enlarged tonsil," she said. "To be on the safe side, I'm sending Andrew to a specialist: a very good ear, nose, and throat doctor who I'm quite certain will get to the bottom of this."

Two days later, another examination, followed by more jotting and nodding.

However, the otolaryngologist's tone and expression seemed especially serious. He pulled off his glasses and rubbed his eyes. "Do you mind if we go into the other room and talk?"

Marci looked uneasily at Jeff and swallowed. *I don't like the way he said "talk,"* she thought. "Wonder what this is about," she whispered as they left the room.

"Could something else be lodged in Andrew's throat?" Jeff whispered back.

Marci turned and smiled at Andrew. "You'll be fine with the nurse. We'll be right back."

Lymphoma? CANCER?

Neither Marci nor Jeff could get past those two frightening words. So much of what the doctor said afterward had gone in one ear and out the other. But then hearing terms like "treatment options" and "success rate" effectively snapped them back to the moment.

"Our first step is removing the tumor," explained the specialist. "And we recommend doing it right away. The color and characteristics of the mass are consistent with non-Hodgkin's lymphoma. Let's get him into surgery on Monday."

"Absolutely," Marci said.

"Whatever we need to do," Jeff agreed.

A week later, both parents sat at another table, this time with an oncologist.

Marci's head was still spinning. *None of this is turning out how I expected. I'd hoped for simple: remove the problem, and that's it.*

Despite a flawless surgery, and though the child was recovering well, the cancer cells had metastasized—were spreading throughout his body. Chemotherapy was now entering the picture.

"We're confident Andrew will beat this," one doctor had said. "There's a high success rate for this type of lymphoma. We've been researching it for twenty years. He will be fine."

It was a ray of hope.

Marci remained calm, vowing to do everything necessary to get through. *It's hard right now, but we* will *get through this. Six months of chemo, and then it will be over.*

Andrew is going to be okay.

※

As the Beyblades skimmed across the arena and the boys high-fived wildly, a pang of fear stabbed at Marci's stomach. Her optimism was being challenged by worry.

Even after all the treatments, there's still the possibility of a relapse.

And then there are the chemo's side effects.
What if something worse happens to him?
How would our kids grow up, knowing they lost their brother?
What is God telling us?
What if we lose him?

THE FEAR-WORRY-STRESS CYCLE

What if?

Whether these two simple words roll off our lips or ripple through our minds, they set into motion our most common form of suffering: a cyclical experience of fear, worry, and stress.

And no one is immune.

For most of us, worry is second nature—often more like a reflex than a choice. On any given day we fret about countless smaller things: whether an accessory matches our outfit, what people will think of us when we open our mouths to speak, about waistlines and wrinkles and workloads. And then plenty of bigger things can hold our thoughts hostage: growing debts and thinly stretched paychecks, protecting our families, strained relationships and social snubs, health scares, parenting challenges, overcoming mistakes, working through painful memories … coming to grips with an unthinkable dilemma.

Just as for the Meyers, it isn't hard to see how we can get caught in a toxic what-if web.

"My wife, kids, and I are Christians," Jeff says, "so we have hope in Jesus Christ. Yet the pain is no less real. My faith and my loved ones are everything to me."

This weary dad talks candidly about a bleak moment right in

the middle of their family trial—a point when the heavy weight of stress was almost too much to bear.

"Andrew began to fight us with the treatments—he didn't want to take his medicine. 'It tastes bad, and I don't like it,' he told me. 'But you have to,' I snapped. 'If you don't take it, you could die.' Suddenly it felt as if the words just hung in the air. I couldn't believe they came out; they shouldn't come from any parent's mouth. That shouldn't be anyone's reality."

Can you relate?

Does anything about Jeff and Marci's struggle read like your story?

An Agonizing Equation: Fear + Worry = Stress

Medical doctors and psychologists agree that worry is a key component of anxiety and chronic stress and that it's often at the heart of so many problems we face: overeating, alcoholism, cigarette smoking, drug abuse, and a long list of other compulsive behaviors. Over the span of our lifetimes, worrying accounts for untold quantities of invaluable time we'll never get back. We even worry about being worried: *Is all this stress killing me?*

Most neuroscientists and psychologists think our brain is actually hardwired to manage stress. They point to early humans who engaged their fight-or-flight instinct daily as a way to survive. Our ancestors used worrisome thoughts as motivators to solve problems, find protection, and prepare for the worst.

Yet in modern times the stuff of sleepless nights and sweaty palms has grown into a loop of unnecessary suffering and is fast becoming a public health crisis. "America is at a critical crossroads when it comes to stress and our health," reports the American

Psychological Association (APA). "Most of us are suffering from moderate to high stress these days, with 44 percent reporting that their stress levels have increased over the past five years."[1]

The so-called "millennials" (broadly, those born between 1979 and 1995) claim higher stress levels than their parents' and grandparents' generations. Of those in this age group—right now there are between seventy-five million and eighty million in the United States—more than half say worry and stress keeps them up at night.[2] Even our nation's youth are fearful. According to the Report of the Surgeon General, anxiety is the most common emotional disorder during childhood and adolescence. About 13 of every 100 children and adolescents ages nine to seventeen experience some kind of anxiety disorder; girls are affected more than boys in about a 2:1 ratio. And, troublingly, even though one-fifth of all children say they "worry a great deal or a lot," only 3 percent of parents rate their children's stress as extreme.[3]

We've observed children as young as three caught up in worry. What's wrong with this picture? Everything! Worried parents raise worried children; this can rob them of emotional well-being. And we're not just talking about nonreligious households. Our research shows that Christians are every bit as worried as the rest of the world.

What triggers worry for most of us? Ten factors:

- Personal finances
- Work-related stresses
- Family
- Parenting
- Relationships

- Health concerns
- Personal safety
- Body image and appearance
- Temptations (including addictions)
- Social acceptance

Nonetheless, there's no reason that circumstances or situations must dictate our peace and our joy any more than our emotions must determine our actions. Worry and anxiety are negatively affecting most and profoundly harming many; it's time for us to learn how to spend each moment more wisely and to establish more quality connections. We need to stop the cycle of worry—and, by God's strength, we can. We *can* begin experiencing the life he wants for us!

All of us who follow Jesus are learning to surrender to the one true Source of peace. He came "that [we] may have life, and have it to the full"[4]—to bring us into intimacy with God, which is foundational to overcoming worry. "Seek first his kingdom and his righteousness," he tells us, "and all these things will be given to you as well. Therefore do not worry about tomorrow, for tomorrow will worry about itself. Each day has enough trouble of its own."[5]

As the Meyers will admit, it's much easier to say we believe these truths than it is to live them out day by day—especially amidst a crisis. Yet their family is managing to do it, and the faithful steps they're taking have been nothing short of transformational.

Let's head back to their story to discover what's making a difference.

What Jeff and Marci Are Learning (and We Can Too)

One evening, while six-year-old Alison was with her grandparents and Andrew was at the hospital undergoing treatments, their oldest son, Nathan (ten), had Jeff all to himself for some much-needed father-son time.

The two loaded up on snacks and watched TV. They talked, and wrestled, and Jeff cracked a few jokes—anything to deflate the stress they'd been feeling. Yet he knew his boy's thoughts were miles away—no doubt in the hospital room, right by Andrew's side.

Nathan, fidgeting with the remote, turned toward his dad. "I need to know something," he said, then paused and glanced away.

"Yes, Son?"

Then he looked Jeff in the eye. "Is Andrew going to die?"

Jeff sighed before responding. "It's so hard. The hardest thing we've ever had to go through. We don't want that to happen. We'll keep praying, and hoping, and doing all we can to fight the illness. But I have to be honest with you, Nathan—"

Now he also paused, fighting emotion, mustering the strength to let out the words. "It's possible—it could happen. It's hard to imagine life without him, but it *could* happen. If he died, you'd have Ally and Mom and me, and we'd keep on loving each other. And we'd be okay."

Jeff smiled and put his hand on the boy's shoulder. "And, guess what? So would Andrew. He'd be in heaven with Jesus. He's a Christian—just like you and our whole family. Jesus loves us and takes care of us and will be with us forever. Hold on to that. Never stop believing it."

A few nights later, Jeff sat on the edge of the bed with his wife, telling her all about his talk with Nathan.

Then he shared another conversation—one he'd had with God.

"Marci," he said tenderly. "I sense the Lord asking me a question. I feel he's asking this of us: 'If I take Andrew away, will you still worship me?'"

She nodded in agreement.

He continued. "I know our faith is being tested—and it's so difficult, so painful. I don't want to lose Andrew—or any of you. I've felt so worried and stressed these past few months. I don't understand why any of this is happening."

He wiped tears from his eyes. Marci squeezed his hand.

"Here's what I said to God," Jeff explained. "I told him, 'Yes, Lord, I will worship you. I will trust you. No matter what you decide to do. All of this is in your hands.'"

Marci opened her Bible to Ephesians 3:20. "Here's what's getting me through this," she said. "'Now to him who is able to do far more abundantly than all that we ask or think, according to the power at work within us, to him be glory in the church and in Christ Jesus throughout all generations, forever and ever. Amen.'"

She then spoke about the many questions swirling through her head—most prominent was, *What are we going to do if we lose Andrew?*—and her own honest conversations with God: "If you take away the most important thing to me—my kids—yes, I will be devastated, but I will not turn my back on you. I know that you love me, and I know you're in control of everything. No matter what you choose, I know there's a reason for it."

She repeated the simple truth Jeff had shared with Nathan: "Jesus takes care of us."

"I know with all my heart that God is going to do something bigger and greater than we can imagine," she said. "Whether he takes Andrew or heals him … he has a purpose for all of this. All we need to do is surrender—and trust. We don't have to waste time in fear, and we don't have to worry about the outcome. Jesus takes care of us!"

Note: As we went to press, Andrew was given a clean bill of health. He is cancer free. He and his friends broke out the Beyblades and Legos and had a fun-filled celebration!

WORRY, ANXIETY, AND STRESS: SIMILAR BUT DIFFERENT

"Are you worried about something?"

"I'm anxious to get going."

"This job is stressing me out!"

We often use *worry, anxiety*, and *stress* interchangeably in everyday conversation. While all three terms describe states we want to avoid, and though they often occur together, they are in fact distinct. Understanding the differences can help us get a better handle on our own situation.

Worry

Here are two psychological definitions of *worry*:

A chain of thoughts and images, negatively affect-laden and relatively uncontrollable.

An attempt to engage in mental problem-solving on an issue whose outcome is uncertain but contains the possibility of one or more negative outcomes.[6]

Emerging research underscores worrying as one of several types of repetitive thought; others include reminiscing, anticipating, and reflecting. Dr. Suzanne Segerstrom, a professor of clinical psychology, has researched repetitive thought among older adults and found that the thoughts vary in terms of whether their content is positive or negative (valence) and whether the tone is of uncertain searching or more certain problem-solving (purpose). Worry typically involves negative thoughts regarding uncertain situations.

Anxiety

Anxiety, typically described more as an emotional state consisting of restlessness, panic, or a sense of impending doom, is often accompanied by physical symptoms like muscle tension, sweating, heart palpitations, and shortness of breath. Anxiety may also include thoughts such as fear of embarrassment or of dying from a heart attack. Anxiety frequently (but not always) arises out of stressful circumstances.

Sometimes people experience anxiety to the extent that they're suffering from an anxiety disorder. Of these there's a wide variety, comprising one of our nation's most common mental health problems. Types include generalized anxiety disorder, obsessive-compulsive disorder, panic disorder, post-traumatic stress disorder, and social phobia (or social anxiety disorder).

Stress

Stress represents this trio's most nebulous term. Dr. Hans Selye, an endocrinologist, coined it in 1936 to describe "the non-specific response of the body to any demand for change."[7] It can refer to external circumstances and also a person's response to those circumstances. Stress can be productive or harmful. For example, the Stressful Life Events Checklist, developed by the psychiatrists Thomas Holmes and Richard Rahe,[8] includes both "positive" and "negative" stress-producing events.

UNDERSTANDING "THE CYCLE"

You'll read about the fear-worry-stress cycle throughout *Seven Secrets of Worry-Free Living*. This isn't an official medical term; we coined it for the sake of clear communication in this book. However, therapists and doctors do often study and refer to specific cycles of worry and anxiety.

For the sake of our discussions in each chapter, we want to ensure that you understand two key factors about the book's primary subject: (1) Worry, anxiety, and negative stress frequently have one thing in common: *fear.* (2) Despite distinctions, they often overlap and sometimes feed on each other.

Here's how we define the fear-worry-stress cycle:

The process whereby a person feels fearful of a particular object or event, worries about encountering that object or situation in the future, experiences a stress reaction, and may then begin to fear and worry about being stressed or worried.

Worry begins with a pang of fear. Thereafter our minds can become stuck on repetitive, negative thoughts about uncertain situations. Eventually this can lead to anxiety and/or harmful stress, and then we may start to fear and worry about the adverse effects of stress on our health.

If you feel trapped somewhere in this cycle, your issue could be physiological, in which case it might be poor nutritional choices or chemical imbalances (such as the overproduction of adrenaline in the brain) causing you to feel anxious. Maybe you're battling a disorder … or maybe your problem is more spiritual in nature; God feels distant to you, and you're struggling to trust him and surrender to his will.

Whether you're grappling with one of these causes or another one, tackling worry, anxiety, and stress in a single book—as you may suspect—is a daunting task. There's a lot to consider, and some aspects can get complicated. To avoid bogging down our conversations with psychobabble, and as a way of helping you get to the root of what's affecting you and those in your care, we will endeavor to walk you through the issues as straightforwardly and engagingly as possible, with strategies, stories, and scripturally based guidance.

Let's get started.

Chapter One

THE SECRET OF WISDOM

Anxious thoughts swirl through our brains when we're tired, when we're sick, when we're crawling through snarled traffic, when we're late for a big meeting. Fear kicks in as our safety is threatened and our circumstances slide out of control. Our brain, on full alert, launches into a fight-or-flight state; adrenaline surges and races everywhere inside us (no need for a highly caffeinated supersized double shot of anything).

The fear-worry-stress cycle is on the rise, in us and in our families. And the research from the Center for Bible Engagement (a division of Back to the Bible) reveals that Christ-followers are every bit as worried as the rest of the world.

- Ben feels trapped by a dead-end job and frets about his future.
- Leslie is panicked about some bad choices her college-age son is making.
- Sarah wonders who will take care of her now that she's eighty—and alone.
- And four-year-old Evan feels so anxious that his teachers don't know how to help. The moment his

mother leaves after bringing him to preschool, immobilizing fear washes over him and holds on tight.

What's going on? A small child's world should be filled with wonder, not inundated with worry. And how can it be that of 2,600 respondents, more than half described themselves as "often worried and fearful"? (As to whether they worry most days of the week, 66 percent of Christian women and 56 percent of Christian men said yes.)

It's partly because of what we've come to expect and accept. Most of us believe it's normal to be busy—frantically racing through day after day, multitasking from deadline to deadline. Combine that with how we've become depersonalized and isolated on our computers and devices, at our jobs, in our communities—even in our homes and our churches. These cultural conditions make commonplace the maladies of stress and anxiety. Something else is at play too: many of us thrive on the excitement of an adrenaline rush, especially those who crave exhilaration and chase after energy that they perceive will spur them to achieve great things.

Yet adrenaline is addictive, and the crashes after the rushes, which our bodies bring about in order to recover, tend to result in persistent fatigue and even depression (much more on this in chapter 5). With worry and stress also in the mix, myriad health problems can arise: dizziness, racing heartbeat, rapid breathing and/or shortness of breath, headache, inability to concentrate, irritability, muscle tension, nausea, nervous energy, and more. Over time, a state of adrenalized anxiety can lead to serious physiological consequences:

- Depressed immune system (making it harder to fight off diseases like cancer)
- Digestive disorders
- Muscle tension
- Increased chances of triggering clinical depression
- Changes in blood chemistry (heightening risk of [for instance] adult-onset diabetes)
- Impairment of the body's ability to form new cells
- Short-term memory loss
- Premature coronary artery disease
- Elevated blood pressure
- Heart failure

At the same time, doctors point out that stress isn't the sole culprit. Actually, stress is just a trigger—it's how we handle stress that matters most. There are effective steps and lifestyle changes every member of the family can take! Christians really do hold the keys to real transformation and meaningful growth. Our lives can be different—less stressful, freer, happier, and far more fulfilling. Our Worry-Wise Plan (we'll get to this in chapter 3) will walk you through a mind-body-spirit approach to finding relief. After identifying the relevant physiological and emotional factors, you can plot a God-centered solution to handling worry.

※

Before we find solutions, though, we've got to understand the problem: what's negatively affecting us and why. As I (Arnie)—along with my research colleague, Dr. Pam Ovwigho—analyzed the spiritual lives of 2,600 Christians, Michael pursued and conducted the interviews for this book. Together we met men, women, and children whose worry tendencies stem from a wide range of difficult struggles, sometimes including panic disorder, obsessive-compulsive disorder (OCD), and post-traumatic stress disorder (PTSD).

In this chapter, we'll dive into the data, explore what worries us, and examine beliefs about worry. Then we'll talk about ways of coping with worry: How do we stop the worry cycle once it's started? Is it possible to sidestep worry altogether? We'll conclude with a focus on the spiritual side of worry.

HOW STRESSED ARE WE?

Since 2007, the American Psychological Association has conducted an annual "Stress in America" survey, which examines how stressed we are, what causes our stress, and how we cope with it. According to the findings of the 2010 APA survey, about half of all adults have experienced a moderate amount of stress in the previous month, and about one in four were extremely stressed.[1]

Those who participated in our study reported similar stress levels. However, there are notable differences by age and gender. Two broad-spectrum examples: the stress that women report feeling is more than what men report, and adults between ages thirty and fifty-nine contend with the highest levels of extreme stress.

Figure 1. Average Stress Level Among U.S. Christians.

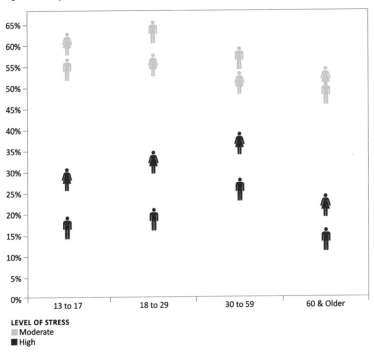

LEVEL OF STRESS
█ Moderate
█ High

WORRY'S MOST FREQUENT FACETS

Ask a couple thousand people what they worry about most and you'll quickly recognize that, whether presently at a high or a low point of stress ("stress-point"), nearly everyone can name something they worry about, even if only occasionally. While details of specific worries certainly vary depending on circumstances, there are themes to what sends most of us into worry mode.

We find many ways to ask *What if?* and then proceed to imagine what could go wrong. Let's explore what these most often center on, at different life stages.

What if … something happens to my family?

Our most frequent worries center on those closest to our hearts, the people we love. Family concerns are by far the most common. This is true overall as well as across genders and across all age groups except tweens. Women do worry about family more than men do, and family worries increase as we age, peaking in the thirty-to-fifty-nine range.

For tweens, family worries focus primarily on their parents—from parents' health to parents' financial concerns. Kids worry that they'll split up, especially when hearing them argue. They also fear their parents won't be proud of them or that circumstances such as parental separation or incarceration would result in their parents not living with them anymore.

Later life stages bring family worries that expand to include emotional health and spiritual concerns as well as physical safety. Believers often question whether certain loved ones will choose to follow Christ. In addition, as we age our worries focus more on children and grandchildren, even though concerns about our parents remain. Sometimes we fret about our relational roles: *Am I a good husband/wife? Am I nurturing my kids as I should?*

> *We are not necessarily doubting that God will do the best for us, we are wondering how painful the best will turn out to be.*
> —*C. S. Lewis*, Into the Wardrobe

The following statements illustrate many of our worries about family:

"I worry about …

"… my family. My infant son was diagnosed with a food allergy, and we've been in the ER twice with him in his first fifteen months, due to severe reaction…. Most of my worry is [from being] constantly on alert to make sure he doesn't eat something he shouldn't."

"… my children and their friendships, if they're associating with Christian friends."

"… my wife potentially cheating on me. I am a stepfather and dealing with the deadbeat that doesn't pay for much of anything, yet he's looked at as a hero by his kids."

"… whether I'm spending enough time with God, family, and others who are important in my life."

"… my family, which encompasses so much: health, finances, shelter, food, clothing, hoping for college for my children."

"… the children in our family, that they would not be drawn away from God into the world. [Also] about our family being healthy and having enough money."

"… my kids—their future (careers, finances, life skills)."

"… my grown children … their walk with God, their finances and health."

"… being a good mom and not neglecting my children's needs. Raising my children in a way that [they] turn out to be 'good,' well-balanced adults."

"… whether my husband and I will ever have children of our own."

"… if my family is going to be restored back to me as the Lord has promised me."

What if … my finances fail?

Current money woes or, even more often, possible future financial problems top the "worry list" for many Christians. Recurrent concerns include being able to meet present family needs (whether employed or experiencing unemployment), managing the finances of a business, holding down a job so as to continue providing, and planning for college or retirement.

Men and women are equally likely to worry about finances. Frequency of financial worry increases with age, again peaking in the thirty-to-fifty-nine-year-old range (often when financial responsibilities are highest) and declining slightly after age sixty.

Respondents in our survey described their money concerns this way:

"I worry about …

"… supporting a family of eight with one income."

"… will we have enough money for future needs?"

"… making the budget for home, ministry, and business needs."

"… paying bills while trying to figure out how to keep my husband from buying more stuff."

"… paying our bills and mortgage as my husband lost his job over a year ago."

"… my job and if I will continue to make enough money to live on."

"… money. I am a single mother with two boys, and I worry that I won't be able to provide for them."

"… money. Owning a business, I worry that it has the money to support the families of our employees. Being a single person, I worry that I have the money to also support myself and pay for medical bills."

"… funding my retirement."

"… always having the money needed to support my family for basic items as well as their college education."

"… having enough money to pay daily bills. I have two jobs and I still come up short every month."

"… finances. I am disabled and the income responsibility rests solely on my husband."

What if … the future doesn't turn out the way I want?

Typically, worry focuses on future events with uncertain outcomes where at least one possible outcome is negative. With so much future ahead of them, it's not surprising to find that worries about the future are fairly common among young adults. One in five eighteen- to twenty-nine-year-olds said they worry about future events and decisions like what college to attend, what career to pursue, and whether they will marry.

"I worry about …

"… the future. I'm a student, always worried about graduating and getting a job."

"… my future and what I'm going to do with my life, how things will work out."

"… my grades at school, what other people think of me, my future. Will I be able to take good care of myself when I leave for college?"

"… what people think of me and [about] my future, specifically who I'll eventually marry."

"… my future. I worry about where I will work after college, will I be doing what I really want in life, will I get married, have kids, complete my bucket list before I die, and those are just the long-term worries. I worry what each day will bring as well."

"… my future. Specifically, how I will balance my career with my husband's and with our desire to start a family. When I have these worries, I try to pray and hand them over to God since I know that he is in charge of my future."

What if … I'm not living my faith as God wants me to?

While younger adults anxiously ponder their future, seniors are more attuned to spiritual matters. On the whole, spiritual issues—whether personal sin, personal spiritual growth, or the spiritual lives of others—don't top many lists of frequent worries. When they do come up, however, they're more likely to be raised by someone sixty or older.

The most common spiritual concern mentioned was personal: Am I following God's will? Am I living in a way pleasing to God?

"I worry about …

    "… if I'm living according to God's will ... not that I'm living a life of sin, but am I living for him in my day-to-day struggles so that he receives the glory? I feel I should be doing so much more but don't know if there is an area of my life I have not surrendered to him yet."

    "… dying before I accomplish the things God needs to do [for me] to become holy."

    "… making sure I'm doing what God needs me to do. Making the most of every opportunity he presents to me to bring him glory!"

    "… whether or not I am having an impact on the world, and God's people, and God's kingdom—[whether or not I am] living with purpose."

    "… failing God, going back to the same sins that trip me up."

WHERE IMAGINATION AND REALITY MEET

Try a brief memory exercise with me. Think about what you were doing exactly one year ago. What happened that day? Did you go to work? Were you at home? On vacation?

Now, here's the second part: What did you worry about that day?

Can you remember?

I've got nothing. Whatever was setting my heart racing and coursing adrenaline through me last year is gone from my memory now. I could probably guess that it was something related to how my kids were doing in school, whether we'd have money left at month's end (or month left at money's end), or my parents' health. But the specifics escape me.

The truth is that most things we worry about either don't happen or, when they do, aren't nearly as bad as we imagined. Certainly there are exceptions, by degree—when a job ends, a biopsy is positive, a child doesn't choose to follow Jesus. It's important to remind ourselves that, by definition, exceptions are instances or cases that don't conform to the usual. Thus, most of the "big" concerns pass out of our minds without becoming reality.

So, then, why do we worry? One main reason is that many of us are uncomfortable with uncertainty. Most people find that uncertainty makes them a little uneasy or stressed. And for about one in four of us, uncertainty produces a great deal of anxiety.

Linking comfort with uncertainty brings us to the spiritual side of worry. God's Word is filled with encouragement to trust him in all circumstances. We have his promises to be with us always, and we have many examples of this promise's guarantee in the lives of the believers who've gone before us. We also have specific examples of God comforting and encouraging his people through uncertainty.

Take Joshua, for example. He'd been Moses' right-hand man, groomed for leadership, and yet the prospect of taking charge of the people seemed to have set his heart racing. This is what the Lord said to him:

> Be strong and courageous, for you shall cause this people to inherit the land that I swore to their fathers to give them. Only be strong and very courageous, being careful to do according to all the law that Moses my servant commanded you. Do not turn from it to the right hand or to the left, that

you may have good success wherever you go. This Book of the Law shall not depart from your mouth, but you shall meditate on it day and night, so that you may be careful to do according to all that is written in it. For then you will make your way prosperous, and then you will have good success. Have I not commanded you? Be strong and courageous. Do not be frightened, and do not be dismayed, for the LORD your God is with you wherever you go.[2]

In these sentences, "Be strong and courageous" appears three times. Yet the point isn't that the Lord tells Joshua to buck up; he's telling him *why* he needn't be worried. Joshua can trust God because God has promised that the land is theirs, and God keeps his promises. He has given Joshua the Book of the Law, and he will be with them every step of the way. Essentially, God is saying that what looks uncertain is actually certain, and so Joshua has no need to worry.

Fast-forward a few thousand years: God is telling us the same thing. It's not as specific as a guarantee that a particular piece of land will be ours, but the message's core is still the same.

∾

Again, worry is a matter of the mind, body, and spirit. Now, it's too simplistic and not helpful to say to anyone, "If you have faith, you won't worry." Actually, it's flat-out wrong.

However, worrying does make a spiritual statement. Our beliefs about who God is—his character, his abilities, his plans—*can* make us more or less prone to worry. We've found that people who trust God more (1) have a higher tolerance for uncertainty and (2) worry less. Similarly, connecting with God through prayer and Scripture also seems to help people accept uncertainty, perhaps by building their trust in him. Other studies likewise have found similar trends.[3]

Later we'll further explore the intersection of spirituality and worry. But first let's consider some other thought processes that can play into the worry cycle.

A LIE WE BELIEVE:
"RESPONSIBLE PEOPLE WORRY"

"Is Gloria worried about starting sixth grade?" asked a well-meaning friend.

"Um … no," Pam stammered. "Errr, not that I've seen, anyway."

"What about you? What about all the peer pressure she'll face and everything?"

There was probably more, but Pam stopped listening at that point. She was too distracted by how unexpected and odd the questions were to her. She hadn't really thought about her usually calm and collected daughter being worried about this. Yes, it was middle school, but she knew almost all the other kids in her grade, was excited about the school, and had breezed through everything academic up to that point.

Then it hit Pam: mother guilt. Within mere minutes, she'd convinced herself that she obviously was a bad mom and should turn in her parent card immediately. She vowed to ask her girl how she was feeling about middle school as soon as they got home. And if she said she was nervous? She'd beg her forgiveness for being clueless.

So how did this happen? One minute Pam was relaxing by the pool, soaking in the last bits of summer. The next she was worried and feeling guilty about not being worried earlier.

Well, unbeknownst to her, lurking in her mind was a positive belief about worry, the belief that responsible people do it. Or, in simpler terms, that worry equals responsible behavior.

Pam is not alone in holding this particular belief. Among those we studied (all of them believers), about three of ten saw some truth in the belief that responsible people worry.

This conviction—an obligation to worry, as it were—is just one of several that psychologists have identified can feed into the worry cycle. For example, some of us believe that fretting is productive. More than two in five of our survey respondents said worrying prompts them to action, helps them know what to do, makes them more effective, and can prevent mishaps from occurring.

Let me briefly illustrate how concern for a problem or situation truly could be productive. Let's use Pam as an example.

When she was leaving home in Pennsylvania to attend school in Maryland, her parents worried that her car would break down along the road and she'd be stranded. So her dad gave her a full starter box of tools and taught her how to check oil, jump-start the battery, and change a tire. Her mom helped her sign up for the American Automobile Association. In short, they turned worry into action. They gave Pam what she needed both to prevent her car from breaking down (to the extent that she could do so) and to get help if it did break down.

Worry *can*, in such a way, be made productive. It can prompt us to deal with a problem or take some type of preventive action.

But problems arise, or keep rising, when we've taken all needful (or even possible) action and still we worry. It's in these types of situations that we may be buying into what we see as worry's "benefits."

Sometimes we use worry as a type of psychological or emotional protection. On some level we believe that if we worry about something, it's less likely to happen. Because worrisome situations often are rife with uncertainty, we tell ourselves that if we fret about them enough, we'll find a way to fix things, to remove the uncertainty and have it all turn out right.

How much do we buy into these myths? Adherence is remarkably common. More than 40 percent of Christians said they believe worry to be effective for problem-solving or avoiding emotional pain at least some of the time. Young people and those who are less spiritually engaged tend to believe more in beneficial aspects of worry than do adults over age thirty and those who are spiritually engaged.

> *Anxiety is not only a pain which we must ask God to assuage but also a weakness we must ask Him to pardon; for He's told us to take no care for the morrow.* —C. S. Lewis, Into the Wardrobe

Not surprisingly, seeing positive value in worry can lead to doing it more. And, if we believe that fretting will solve a problem or diminish the pain it's causing, why would we not continue doing it? However, that logic falls apart when we consider other aspects of the matter. For one thing, chronic worrying hurts our bodies and our spirits. For another, most situations we worry about contain factors beyond our control.

WORRY CAN MAKE ME SICK …
WHICH *REALLY* MAKES ME WORRY

Perhaps the notion that worry can be beneficial sounds to you as wacky as hearing that it's helpful to wear a full-length mink coat for scuba diving. Either way, chances are pretty good that you've picked up this book because you're concerned about the harm that worry causes. Do you believe in the truth of any or all of these statements?

I could make myself sick from worrying.

Worrying puts my body under a lot of stress.

Worry can make it hard to see a situation clearly.

A conviction that worry is harmful or gets in the way of handling a situation represents a negative belief about worry. Worry does indeed affect us negatively (body, mind, and spirit), so it's not surprising that most Christ-followers hold strongly to beliefs like these. We found that 93 percent affirm that at least one of these three declarations is true.

Understanding the harm of worry can help us if it compels us to reject worrying in the first place or to stop the worry cycle once it's started. But sometimes the fact of its damaging effects just feels like another thing to worry about. Clinical psychologist Adrian Wells, who refers to this as "Type 2" worry, has found that worrying about worry is a key contributor to anxiety.[4]

The bottom line, then, is to be aware of these effects without letting that awareness paralyze you. If reminding yourself that worry is unhelpful and injurious stops you from worrying, then it's a good coping strategy for you, one to keep using. If thinking about how destructive worry can be gets you worrying about worrying, then it's time to remove this from your coping box and find some other, more helpful tools.

What if … worrying means I lack faith?

I know worrying is a sin because it means not trusting that God will work out my life. He holds my future in his hands. I struggle the most with worrying, and I think it keeps me from having a true relationship with God because I don't trust him like I should.   —Brianna

We've mentioned our discomfort with uncertainty and thinking patterns that contribute to worry. We've also noted that another significant piece of the worry puzzle is the spiritual. Most of us are familiar with Jesus telling his disciples to not worry because God would care for them—how would he not do so, when clearly he cares for the sparrows and for the lilies of the field? Accordingly, most Christians hold worry to be a sin.

Our study participants identified a number of worry's spiritual effects. A substantial portion feel that worrying indicates a lack of faith and feel guilty when they worry. Even more believe worry to be displeasing to God and an inhibitor to spiritual growth.

Uncertainties and beliefs—how do they all fit together?
What impact do they have on how much and how often we worry?

Recognizing that too much focus on our concerns may get in the way of our relationship with the Lord could prompt us to seek him more. Spiritual activities (such as prayer, worship, and reading God's Word) may then break the worry cycle and provide comfort. But over-focus upon or obsession with how worry is displeasing to God may lead us to fret about whether he still loves us or to anxiously fear that he will abandon us. The goal of focusing on the truth is not to become and remain mired in our faithlessness and insufficiency but rather to remind us of—and root us in—the Lord's faithfulness and sufficiency.

Our Research Says ...

- Older adults use spiritual coping techniques like prayer and meditating on Scripture more than younger adults and teens do.

- Teens are more likely than older adults to question God's love for them when bad things happen.

- Women worry more than men about family members. Two in five women listed family as their most frequent worry, compared to 28 percent (just over one in four) of men.

Recap and Reflect

Talking Points for Couples or Group Study

▶ Analysis of CBE's research—coupled with findings from other trustworthy national studies—reveals that worry among families is at an all-time high. And the experts we talked to insist our nation is moving toward a related public health crisis. "America is at a critical crossroads when it comes to stress and our health," says the APA's CEO, Dr. Norman B. Anderson. "Worry is also taking a toll on kids. Almost a third of children reported that they had experienced a physical health symptom often associated with stress, such as headaches, stomachaches, or trouble falling or staying asleep. And get this: parents often don't realize their own stress is affecting their children."

▶ Consider these common worries among parents, kids, and millennials.[5] Check those that apply to you and your family.

What Husbands Worry About:

☐ *How can I calm the fears of my worried wife?*

☐ *How can I protect my family?*

☐ *Why can't I connect with my kids?*

☐ *Is my job safe?*

☐ *Will the economy take another nosedive?*

☐ *Am I normal sexually? (Why do I lack energy?)*

☐ *Is my marriage okay?*

☐ *Is my health okay?*

☐ *What if I die? (How will my family survive?)*

☐ *Why don't I sense direction for my life?*

☐ *Why am I bored with church?*

☐ *Why does my spiritual life feel so stuck?*

What Wives Worry About:

☐ *How can I help my stressed-out husband?*

☐ *How can I protect my kids?*

☐ *What kind of a future will my children have?*

☐ *Will we ever make ends meet?*

☐ *What if a family member gets sick? (Can we afford the bills?)*

☐ *Why do I feel so angry and bitter all the time?*

☐ *Am I attractive enough to my husband?*

☐ *Why won't my husband give me the attention I need?*

☐ *Why can't I get along with my in-laws?*

☐ *What do others think of me?*

☐ *How can I help my aging parents?*

☐ *Are we pursuing God's will for our lives?*

What Kids and Teens Worry About:

☐ *Why do Mom and Dad fight a lot?*

☐ *Am I a disappointment to my parents?*

☐ *Do my parents love me? (Do they love each other?)*

☐ *Does God love me?*

- ☐ *What if I don't make it to heaven?*
- ☐ *Am I safe?*
- ☐ *What if somebody dies?*
- ☐ *Will I fail at school?*
- ☐ *Do the other kids like me?*
- ☐ *Is my body normal?*
- ☐ *Am I smart enough, attractive enough?*
- ☐ *What kind of a future will I have?*

What the Millennial Generation Worries About:

- ☐ *Will I ever have enough money to live on?*
- ☐ *Will I get a decent job—the kind I prepared for in grad school?*
- ☐ *Why do my parents and I disagree on so many issues?*
- ☐ *Am I attractive to the opposite sex?*
- ☐ *How can I hope to ever be married when I'm constantly rejected now?*
- ☐ *Will my marriage survive? (My spouse and I fight all the time.)*
- ☐ *Will I ever figure out who I am and what I believe?*
- ☐ *Does God really love me?*
- ☐ *Why am I so depressed all the time?*

   ❋ Pick a few statements that you checked and talk about them together.

Chapter Two

THE SECRET
OF SELF-AWARENESS

Not everyone gets to wake up with a clear head and a calm heart. The fact is, most of us struggle with emotional and physical pain of some kind, and we're often distracted and dismayed by the many what-if questions that worry us. Nevertheless, relief is within reach—for every age, for every stage of life, and for every member of the family.

The first step is becoming self-aware and making an effort to learn what's going on inside our bodies. Specifically, we must grasp the adrenaline connection to worry.

Adrenaline is one of the most powerful chemicals either man-made or naturally occurring. *Adrenaline is pure speed!* According to Dr. Eric T. Scalise, anytime we feel excited or anxious, the brain tells the adrenal glands—which sit on the back of our kidneys—to release adrenaline to manage that stress. But our brain doesn't distinguish between a joyful moment and a life-threatening crisis. Adrenaline rushes through us as we encounter *any* kind of excitement, from the loss of someone we love to the birth of a child.

On the upside, an adrenaline rush can be exhilarating and

can give us the energy and clarity we need to achieve whatever is needed. On the downside, the exhilaration can be addicting, and it can plunge us into a cycle of fear, worry, and stress.

Let's take a closer look.

THE NEUROBIOLOGY OF STRESS

Our brain is part chemical factory, part German autobahn.

Information is transmitted from one nerve cell to the next by chemical messengers called *neurotransmitters*. They race through the nerves, giving orders: "Full alert—get moving," or "Be calm and slow down." They tell the brain to be happy, sad, anxious, or tranquil. They warn of emergencies and indicate when it's safe for us to rest.

How—by what process? Through *stress hormones*, pumped into the bloodstream.

Each nerve cell (or neuron) releases small amounts of neurotransmitters, some of which trigger a reaction in the next neuron and some of which are reabsorbed by the original neuron (in a process known as *reuptake*).[1] The subsequent effects on our body depend on factors including the type of neurotransmitter released, the amount that's produced or reabsorbed, the sensitivity of the receptors on the receiving neuron, and the location in the brain where the process is occurring.[2]

Two hormones play a big role in the adrenaline-stress connection: GABA (gamma-aminobutyric acid), or what Dr. Archibald Hart, a licensed psychologist and an expert on this subject, calls a "happy messenger," and cortisol, which he calls a "sad messenger."[3] We need both neurotransmitter types to coexist and work in tandem inside our brains. When we're ill, sad messengers tell the body to rest. When our lives are endangered, they act as lifesavers, sending our body into action to prevent harm. And happy messengers help us to cope with pain and remain tranquil; they energize us and make us feel vital and optimistic.

Excessive worry and anxiety, however, cause the body's sympathetic nervous system to release large amounts of cortisol. This can boost blood sugar levels and triglycerides (blood fats) that the body can use for temporary fuel. "Cortisol is kind of like the after-burner," Scalise explains. "It gives everything a good kick. But too much can be a problem."[4]

GABA

- Chief inhibitory neurotransmitters in the central nervous system (CNS)
- Regulates neuronal excitability and helps us to calm down
- Includes brain chemicals such as serotonin, dopamine, norepinephrine (noradrenaline)

Cortisol

- Partners with adrenaline
- Is released in response to stress
- Depletes GABA

The Fight-or-Flight Reaction

Every time adrenaline is released in the body, the brain signals the blood supply to go to our major muscle groups. Why? To help us determine if we should engage or disengage from a given situation—in other words, should we fight for our lives or head for the hills? But, as blood is pumped to our muscles, think about where it isn't going: to our brains. Or, in a sense, messages are being steered from its thinking portion to its feeling realm. That's why a stressful situation often sparks emotions that can include fear, panic, anger, distrust, and insecurity.

From "High Alert" to "System Crash"

When our adrenaline hormones are exhausted from overuse, our bodies crash; adrenaline is then underproduced in an attempt to recover from its overproduction. With underproduction of adrenaline during such times, we can feel so vulnerable that even the smallest stressor might seem overwhelming. Each of our physiological systems interacts with the others and is profoundly influenced by our coping style and our psychological state.

When the GABA and cortisol hormones are in balance, we usually feel pretty good—relatively peaceful, happy, tranquil. But when the sad messengers outnumber the happy ones, we end up depressed, panicked, worried, and/or anxious. Says Dr. Hart:

> I am truly amazed by this process. Proper communication between our brain cells is all wonderfully complex and vitally essential to our sanity. Normal human emotions are determined by whether these neurotransmitters are successful in communicating their messages to your brain cells. On a typical day in the life of your brain, literally trillions of messages are sent and received by these neurotransmitters.[5]

STRESS MANAGEMENT IS THE KEY

So, with this "neuro snapshot" in mind, let's approach the process of how to handle it. The next step involves asking a key question: Why is my life, and/or the life of my family, being supercharged with so much adrenaline?

Then, look around. (Go on—try it.) What do you see … at home, at the office, at school, at church? Would you describe you and your family as "adrenaline junkies," busy people zooming through activities and taking on more and more projects and tasks to the point of overcommitment and then exhaustion?

To recap our conversation above, the sympathetic nervous system (SNS) turns on the fight-or-flight response, and the parasympathetic nervous system (PNS) promotes the relaxation response. The SNS and PNS maintain metabolic equilibrium by making adjustments whenever anything disturbs this balance. So our goal is *homeostasis*—the state of metabolic equilibrium between our body's stimulating and tranquilizing chemical forces. Another way to state our goal is, "Let's find balance again."

The question is, how? Once worry triggers an anxious state, how do we get our bodies to return to normal, that is, get the tranquilizing parasympathetic nervous system to calm things down? The answer is not stress *elimination* but stress *management*. This means learning how to take steps that will effectively help our brains to activate the relaxation response.

And the Bible offers some clues:

"That is why I tell you not to worry about everyday life— whether you have enough food and drink, or enough clothes to wear. Isn't life more than food, and your body more than clothing? Look at the birds. They don't plant or harvest or store food in barns, for your heavenly Father feeds them. And aren't you far more valuable to him than they are? Can all your worries add a single moment to your life?"[6]

Christ's Sermon on the Mount gives us an expansive picture of how our lives as his followers should look. He speaks of our being "salt" and "light," of caring for the needy, of prayer and fasting before addressing money and possessions. Then, on our tendency to worry, Jesus gently reminds us that fretting is just plain pointless. God, our Father, knows what we need, loves us, and will care for us. Yes, life presents uncertainties. But while we don't have ultimate control, we know who does, and he's always focused on what's best for us. And the last question in Christ's words above gets to the heart of why worry is pointless: *it changes nothing.*

This is why we're committed to helping you free yourself and your family from worry. It's important early on to take some time to assess how much you actually worry. In this chapter, you'll find a few tools to help you gauge not only this but also what triggers might set off a worry cycle and what thought patterns may keep you in it. We call this information your "worry profile." Further, you can help your spouse, kids, and other loved ones complete their own profiles, and later in the book we'll show how to use worry profiles to develop each person's own customized action plan for worry-free living.

MY WORRY PROFILE:
HOW MUCH DO I FEEL WORRIED?

God created each of us uniquely. Some are naturally "cool cucumbers" that seem to pass through even the most troubling times with little anxiety. Others are racked with worries around the clock, with little relief and few periods of calm. Most experience life somewhere in between these two extremes, with seasons of anxiety and worry and seasons of peace and tranquility.

When should we be concerned? One main criterion in psychopathology is that the conditions interfere with a person's life. When moods or behaviors start impacting work or relationships, there is a need to seek help.

Our first worry-profile tool focuses on how much you worry. The goal is to give you a handle not only on the frequency of your worry but also on the extent to which worry is affecting your life. If you are being heavily impacted, it may be time to get some outside help (for instance, beginning with talking to your doctor and/or pastor).

Please read each question below and circle how often it has been true of you in the past month.

	Never	Somtimes	Often	Always
In any given situation, I imagine how things can go wrong.	0	1	2	3
No matter what I do, I can't get my mind off my problems.	0	1	2	3

	Never	Somtimes	Often	Always
I worry no matter my circumstances.	0	1	2	3
I know I shouldn't worry about things, but I can't help it.	0	1	2	3
My worries overwhelm me.	0	1	2	3
I find myself worrying about something.	0	1	2	3
I think about how the world is a dangerous place.	0	1	2	3
I avoid certain activities or places because they make me too nervous.	0	1	3	4
My worries hold me back from doing things I'd like to do.	0	1	3	4
My family complains that I worry too much.	0	1	2	3
I have trouble going to sleep or staying asleep because of worry.	0	1	2	3
I experience headaches, stomach pain, and/or digestive problems because of worry.	0	1	2	3
Add the numbers you circled in each column:				
Now add the total from each column to get your score:				

What does my score mean?

If your score is 12 or lower, you have a *mild* level of worry. While you may occasionally worry, you don't feel overwhelmed by it; it's not greatly affecting your life. The rest of this book is full of tips that can enable you keep worry in check and help you help others with their worry.

If your score is between 13 and 21, you have a *moderate* level of worry. Although it may not always overwhelm you, worry can be a problem for you. It's particularly important that you use the strategies outlined in part 3 to reduce your worry and to prevent it from worsening.

If your score is 22 or higher, you have a *severe* level of worry. Still, even if you feel your worry is uncontrollable, there is hope. Part 3 will assist you in crafting a customized plan for taming the worry beast. It's also a good idea to consult your doctor to see if any physiological problems are contributing to the troubles you're experiencing.

MY WORRY PROFILE:
HOW DO I RESPOND TO UNCERTAINTY?

As we saw in chapter 1, how comfortable you are with uncertainty plays a big role in your susceptibility to worry. Nearly all of our what-if scenarios contain at least some element of uncertainty, whether it's in regard to the outcome, the timeline, or both. Our next tool asks you to reflect on how you typically deal with uncertainty.

	Never	Sometimes	Often	Always
When things are uncertain, I feel nervous, anxious, or unsettled.	0	1	2	3
Unforeseen events greatly upset me.	0	1	2	3

	Never	Sometimes	Often	Always
Ambiguity stresses me out.	0	1	2	3
My mind can't relax until I know what will happen tomorrow.	0	1	2	3
I can't stop thinking about a situation when I'm not sure how it will turn out.	0	1	2	3
Add the numbers you circled in each column:				
Now add the total from each column to get your score:				

What does my score mean?

If your score is 5 or lower, you're *comfortable* with uncertainty. This means life's unknowns don't generally stress you out, which tends to set you up to worry less.

If your score is between 6 and 11, you're *somewhat comfortable* with uncertainty. Not knowing how a situation will turn out or what will happen next can raise your heart rate a bit and may give you moments or seasons of worry. At those times, it would be helpful to apply some of the strategies you'll find in part 3.

If your score is 12 or higher, you're *very uncomfortable* with uncertainty. Life's unknowns create high anxiety and leave you worrying over a long list of what-ifs. Actively working to strengthen your ability to deal with uncertainty, including reminders to yourself of God's presence and power, will help you lower your daily stress and weather future uncertainties.

MY WORRY PROFILE:
HOW DO I THINK ABOUT WORRY?

Your profile is almost complete! We hope that as you've gone through the previous sections you've learned about your worry tendencies and levels of comfort with uncertainty. How you think about worry—whether it's helpful, to what degree it's harmful, etc.—provides the third segment. In chapter 1 we broached some of these beliefs and how they can feed the worry cycle. Now it's time to reflect on your own beliefs. Read each statement below and indicate how it does or doesn't reflect your convictions.

	No	Yes
I worry in order to know what to do.	0	1
If I've already worried about a situation, then I'll be able to handle it better if it turns out badly.	0	1
Worrying can prevent mishaps from occurring.	0	1
I know I shouldn't worry about things, but I can't help it.	0	1
Worrying motivates me to do the things I must do.	0	1
Worrying helps me find solutions to my problems.	0	1
Responsible people worry.	0	1
Total how many of these you answered with yes:		
I could make myself sick with worrying.	0	1
Worrying puts my body under a lot of stress.	0	1
Worry can keep me from seeing a situation clearly.	0	1
Total how many of these you answered with yes:		

	No	Yes
My worrying is a sign that I lack faith.	0	1
Worrying is a sin.	0	1
I feel guilty when I worry.	0	1
My worrying is displeasing to God.	0	1
Total how many of these you answered with yes:		

What do my scores mean?

The first seven statements reflect positive underlying beliefs about worry. The more you agree with these, the more likely you are to accept or even embrace worry. The next three statements focus on negative beliefs about worry. If you agree with them, you're at risk of getting tied up in secondary worry. That is, you may find you start worrying about a situation and then become more and more anxious as you start worrying about being worried. An important facet of your worry-wise strategy will be learning how to stop the worry cycle before it escalates (we'll get into this strategy in chapters 3 through 5).

The last four statements concern spiritual beliefs about worry. If they prompt you to seek God through prayer and his Word, they're productive. However, if you find that they feed your worry, causing anxiety about your spiritual life, addressing them should be part of your strategy.

A WORRY PROFILE FOR MY YOUNG CHILD

Many young children also struggle with worry, but it can be hard for them to verbalize what's troubling them. Depending

THE SECRET OF SELF-AWARENESS · 57

on your child's age, maturity, and reading ability, you might have him/her read and answer the questions, or you may need to read and explain or illustrate the items. (In two sidebars below—"A Checklist for Anxious Behavior" and "Reading the Worry Signs"—you'll be able to consider and hopefully, if need be, ascertain whether your child is showing signs of anxious behavior.)

In the past two weeks, how often have you been bothered by these problems?

	Not at all	Several days	More than half the days	Nearly every day
Not being able to sleep or to control my worrying	0	1	2	3
Becoming easily annoyed or irritable	0	1	2	3
Feeling nervous, anxious, or on edge	0	1	2	3
Feeling afraid, as if something awful might happen	0	1	2	3
Worrying too much about various things	0	1	2	3
Having trouble relaxing	0	1	2	3
Being so restless that it's hard to sit still	0	1	2	3
Add the numbers you circled in each column:				
Now add the total from each column to get your child's score:				

What does his/her score mean?

If your child's score is 9 or lower, he/she has a *minimal* anxiety level. Worry is not a big issue right now. Together you can use the tips in chapter 9 to keep worries at bay as he/she navigates toward the teenage years.

If your child's score is between 10 and 14, he/she has a *moderate* level of anxiety—even if he/she isn't feeling overwhelmed, worry is starting to become a problem. You can help reduce worry and prevent it from worsening by adopting strategies outlined in part 3.

If your child's score is 15 or higher, he/she has a *severe* level of anxiety, experiencing worry that feels out of control and needing you to help him/her to break free from the worry cycle. The strategies in part 3 will help you craft a plan together. Also, consult your pediatrician to evaluate whether or not a medical condition might be contributing to the anxiety.

READING THE WORRY SIGNS

In Baton Rouge, Louisiana, Jennifer is confused. Her nine-year-old, Olivia, has retreated to her bedroom after barely touching supper.

What's happened to my little chatterbox? She barely takes a breath between stories about her favorite bands and books … and girl gossip. And she can never get enough of my cooking. Something isn't right with her.

Several hundred miles away, in Portland, Maine, John is trying to figure out why his eleven-year-old won't shoot hoops or do anything else with him. Lately, Ethan just hasn't been the same happy kid, usually eager to hang out with the family.

"It's like we're raising Dr. Jekyll and Mr. Hyde," he tells his wife. "He's withdrawn and sad—like he's seriously stressing over something. The question is, *what*?"

A CHECKLIST OF ANXIOUS BEHAVIOR

Suspect your child is struggling with worry?
Look for these signs:

- ☐ Frequent crying
- ☐ Frequent headache and/or upset stomach
- ☐ Lack of interest in once-loved activities
- ☐ Inability to look an adult in the eye
- ☐ Inability to stay focused or to concentrate
- ☐ Withdrawal from social interactions
- ☐ Sudden drop in grades
- ☐ Refusal to go to school
- ☐ Constant restlessness
- ☐ Problems going to bed and staying asleep
- ☐ Feeling tired and worn out nearly all day every day
- ☐ *For Teens:* Battling with heavy guilt or shame on a daily basis
- ☐ *For Teens:* Feelings of worthlessness—to the point of not being able to function with a positive demeanor
- ☐ *For Teens:* Weight loss (without trying to lose) or weight gain (more than 5 percent of body weight in one month), loss of appetite or increased appetite
- ☐ *For Teens:* Self-medication with alcohol or other substances

Both parents have reason to be alarmed. While an abrupt change in behavior feels like an hourly occurrence in the lives of teenagers, in young children, and tweens it's often the first clue that they may be worried about something.

"A talkative kid who clams up for days, or is on a pendulum swing from happy to sad, should be taken seriously by parents," says Tess Cox, a pediatric physician assistant in Colorado Springs. "Children cope with worry and anxiety in very different ways from adults."[7] So, for one thing, we shouldn't merely interpret their apparent feelings through the lens of our own emotions. Here are some other signs to look for.

For Young Kids

Soiling. This is a classic red flag for children who've been potty trained. If there isn't a medical problem—such as a urinary tract infection—there is probably an issue with worry, or possibly he/she has gone through something distressing or traumatic.

For All Kids

Sudden changes in appetite. Some children are picky eaters. But we should be concerned if they suddenly refuse to eat something they used to enjoy. Emotional eating (particularly snacks and junk food) can also be pointing to a problem.

Sudden changes in sleep patterns, especially if they aren't sleeping through the night. Sleep disturbance can be a big clue that something's wrong. At times, most children will fight sleep.

But parents should take note if it's recurring or if children have nightmares and bad dreams more often than occasionally.

Expressions of sadness. Some young children are able to verbalize well how they feel. "Maybe this is a result of our digital age," says Dr. Trina Young-Greer, a licensed clinical psychologist and director of Genesis Counseling Center, "but I'm often amazed at how a four-year-old is sometimes able to tell me, 'I'm sad. I'm upset.'"[8] It's plain that if your child expresses sadness in this way, you need to listen and tune in to what's going on. The goal is to get to the root of why he/she is worried.

For Teenagers

Major depressive disorder. Here are some symptoms teens will commonly experience if they have a major depressive disorder. Someone with this condition will experience at least five of these symptoms for more than two weeks in such a way that it interferes with daily life.

- Irritable or sad most of the day or all day long
- No longer interested in once-loved activities
- Weight loss (without trying to lose) or weight gain (more than 5 percent of body weight in one month), loss of appetite or increased appetite
- Not being able to sleep or sleeping too much nearly every day
- Feeling tired and worn out nearly all day every day
- Restlessness
- Battling with heavy guilt on a daily basis

- Feelings of worthlessness—to the point of not being able to function with a positive demeanor
- Lack of ability to concentrate or make decisions

❧

Knowledge is the first step toward finding relief from worry. The basic helps in this chapter are meant to provide you with specific knowledge about how much your family members worry and what thoughts may be contributing to that worry.

However, a word of caution: Because our beliefs about worry and faith can contribute to the worry cycle, many of us can be tempted to think, *it's all in my head*. That is *not* the case. When working through our struggles or helping a loved one who's suffering, the last things anyone should hear are messages like, "Get over it and have more faith," "Stop being so self-absorbed and start thinking about the needs of others," or "Worry is nothing short of idolatry."

Our Research Says . . .

- Chronic worrying can interfere with your appetite, sleep, job performance, and relationships.
- It's estimated that more than six million Americans suffer from panic attacks. Symptoms of a panic attack, such as shortness of breath and a pounding heart, are often mistaken for a heart attack.[9]
- One out of three people with panic disorder subsequently develop agoraphobia. The good news is that early diagnosis and treatment of panic disorder can shorten its chronicity and reduce a person's chances of developing agoraphobia.

THE SECRET OF SELF-AWARENESS • 63

Recap and Reflect
Talking Points for Couples or Group Study

❱ Family life can be turbulent, and we'll all have our share of troubles in a given day—including worrisome thoughts that invade our minds. Being concerned won't hurt us; the problem arises when we allow anxiety to paralyze our thinking.

✺ Share what you learned from your worry profile. *How did my family and I score? Is this what I anticipated? Am I surprised or concerned?*

❱ As we said earlier, becoming self-aware—learning about what's bugging us and examining how we react to stress—can move us toward worry-free living. Our intent here is *not* to dispense a medical diagnosis. (That's a conversation we hope you'll have with a medical professional.) Rather, now is the time to think about your next steps. With knowledge on your side, you're better able to pray, plan, and plot a realistic course toward healing.

✺ Identify at least two issues you want to work on and help with in the lives of those in your care. *How does a commitment to progress make me feel?* (e.g., motivated, nervous, hopeful, overwhelmed, inspired ...)

Chapter Three

THE SECRET OF RIGHT THINKING
(Calming Our Mind)

While we've identified many worry- and anxiety-related problems, now it's time to shift our conversation toward meaningful solutions. In this chapter (and continuing through chapters 4 and 5), we want to help you either get on or continue along that road toward healing. Our goal is to walk with you through a practical and effective mind-body-spirit approach to handling worry—what we call the "Worry-Wise Plan."

Straightaway, let's be clear about what this plan is and isn't.

It could be that the second you read phrases like *mind-body-spirit,* you can't help thinking, *Uh-oh—is this book suddenly taking a New Age turn?* Or maybe the title "The Secret of Right Thinking" is sending you in the opposite direction: *Here come the impossible standards that normal people can't live up to.*

Rest assured—you'll find no crazy concepts here.

We don't follow the "Transcendentalist's Metaphysical Playbook for Enlightenment and Holistic Happiness" any more than we see ourselves as the "poster children" for Christianity. We're merely Christ-followers and ministry professionals—one a behaviorist and researcher (Arnie) and the other a journalist and author (Michael). During our many decades on planet Earth, we've both learned that it's a big mistake to turn to other people or to manmade philosophies in an effort to quench a thirsty spirit or to find emotional healing and wholeness. Those who attempt this are always deluded, ever disappointed. We can find life only in God's Living Spirit. Right thinking and emotional wellness don't come about through mechanistic rituals or by filling our minds with positive thoughts or correct theology. This is nurtured through relationship with a Person.

Theology doesn't save. Manmade philosophies can't save. *Only Jesus Christ saves.*

"The first-century disciples were totally involved with a Person," explains Richard Halverson in *No Greater Power.* "They were followers of Jesus. They were learners of Jesus. They were committed to Jesus."[1] Our faith grows as we encounter Jesus in the Bible. Scripture's message is the message of Jesus, who said, "I am the way and the truth and the life."[2] Therefore, our Worry-Wise Plan is grounded in the guidance we can trust: the common-sense principles found in God's timeless, holy Word.

The Bible makes it clear what medical professionals are now echoing: our mind, body, and spirit are interconnected. For example, obviously I inhabit a physical body, and my body's health is connected to my feelings and thoughts. So from a behavioral health perspective, I know I need to treat my *entire* body. Obsessive thoughts—the judgmental ones and the negative self-talk that goes on inside my head—can affect how I feel. This, in turn, can affect my body.

Consider the stomach, which can act as a "second brain" when it comes to worrying. According to Dr. Mehmet Oz, like our brains, "our stomachs have their own nervous systems, called the enteric nervous system. When we worry, millions of receptors embedded in the gastrointestinal tract react to fear by speeding up or slowing down our digestion, which can lead to nausea, diarrhea, and heartburn."[3]

Elouise Renich Fraser says this about our physical bodies and the effects of worry:

> My body, once ignored and despised, has become an ally in the reorientation of my internal and external life. It lets me know when I'm running away, avoiding yet another of God's invitations to look into my past and the way it binds me as a theologian. I can't trust my mind as often as I trust my body. My mind tries to talk me into business as usual, but my body isn't fooled. Insomnia, intestinal pain, and diarrhea let me know there's work to be done.[4]

Let's dig in and discover how to apply the Worry-Wise Plan to our own circumstances. Remember, we want to unravel wrong thinking/negative thoughts and begin managing worry. We'll need to accomplish this on three interrelated levels: our mind, our body, and our spirit.

In the paragraphs that follow, we'll focus on our mind.

YOUR MIND'S WORRY-WISE PLAN

We can break the fear-worry-stress cycle by calming our thoughts. We need to clue in to the neurological processes at work and then take steps to help us quiet our brain and worry less. First, understand that worry is much more than a "feeling." Dr. Oz explains that deep inside our brain is an almond-shaped structure called the amygdala, which acts as our fear-and-anxiety center. "When we experience a potential worry, the amygdala sends warning messages to the cortex, the rational part of our brain, which can assess whether that worry is of true concern. As the rational cortex is flooded with more and more warning signals from the amygdala, however, it is unable to process them all, leading to worry loops or anxiety."[5]

Here's where to start:

Identify Your Degree of Stress

From a clinical perspective, anxiety and worry are on a continuum: On one end is someone who may be nervous and upset about an issue but can think rationally about it. On the other end is someone in the grip of a full-on panic attack: her heart is racing and she feels as if she can't breathe.

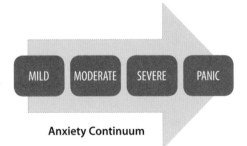

Anxiety Continuum

Here's a look at four different levels of anxiety.

Mild: This is the stuff of everyday life—a pang of worry here, a surge of stress there. No one is immune, and it isn't necessarily a negative experience. Again, a little bit of adrenaline and stress can motivate us to take action, to run for safety, to complete a task—and, because our perception is increased, mild anxiety can enhance creativity and out-of-the-box problem-solving.

What Happens at This Level
- Slight Shortness of Breath
- Elevated Pulse and Blood Pressure
- Stomach Discomfort

Recommended Action: Follow the steps presented in this chapter, emphasizing diet changes, aerobic exercise, and relaxation techniques.

Moderate: At this point our minds get increasingly stuck on worried, what-if thinking. *What if I look foolish in front of my coworkers? What if the doctor gives me really bad news? What if I fail the test?* Yet a moderate anxiety level is still considered normal by healthcare professionals. Despite having a narrowed perceptual field, we're still able to solve problems and work through what's bugging us.

What Happens at This Level
- Sweating
- Shaky Voice
- Headache
- Trouble Sleeping

Recommended Action: Follow the steps presented in this chapter, emphasizing diet changes, aerobic exercise, and relaxation techniques.

Severe: This degree of anxiety begins to interfere with our lives. Often we feel overwhelmed by fearful thoughts, and awareness of our surroundings is significantly narrowed; we simply can't take our mind off what's stressing us. *I can't handle this alone,* we think (and increasingly believe). *I just don't know what to do.*

What Happens at This Level

- Muscle Tension
- Hyperventilation
- Talking Fast in a High Tone
- Pacing
- Trembling

Recommended Action: Follow the steps presented in this chapter and seek the advice of a healthcare professional as well as a Christian counselor or pastor.

Panic: This degree of anxiety—the highest and most dangerous—can be a terrifying experience. Sufferers often sense impending doom, and they may be unable to speak logically or hold a thought (can't think rationally). Some pace uncontrollably and become increasingly active without a purpose. Intervention is crucial, as prolonged panic can be harmful to one's health.

What Happens at This Level

- Extreme Muscle Tension
- Pronounced Shortness of Breath; Often Gasping for Air
- Rapid Pulse and Elevated Blood Pressure
- Aimless and Haphazard Actions
- Shaking

Recommended Action: Seek medical attention (both from your family physician and from a licensed therapist), gain some spiritual advice from a pastor or church leader, and consider following the steps presented in this chapter.

MY WORRY-WISE PLAN:
The Degree of Anxiety in My Life

Here's how I would rate my degree of anxiety:

☐ Mild   ☐ Moderate   ☐ Severe   ☐ Panic

Here's how I feel when anxiety strikes:

Get Grounded

Whenever our degree of anxiety maxes out, we must talk ourselves down from a "panic cliff." And then we can get moving toward truth and more constructive thinking.

"I strive to walk patients step-by-step through these kinds of circumstances," Christian therapist Nanette Gingery Lankas explains. "I tell them something like this: 'You're in my office. Grab on to the arm of the chair and look around. You're safe. Everything is okay. Take a deep breath, and let's work on slowing the breathing.' I get them to the point in which the anxiety is manageable."[6]

As Nanette suggests, getting grounded is a technique that an individual can do on his own. I (Michael) have used this exercise after waking in the middle of the night, panicked about something. When my heart is racing and my head is swirling with all kinds of anxious thoughts, I stop and I remind myself that it's the middle of the night. *Everything seems worse when it's dark out. Let's take some time to breathe, to relax, and then go back to bed.* And then I do that as needed.

MY WORRY-WISE PLAN:
Attacking Panic

(1) Take deep breaths and slow your heart rate.

(2) Hold on to something—the edge of a chair, your Bible, a photo . . . anything.

(3) Examine your surroundings. What do you see?

(4) Remind yourself to be still and to trust God.[7] Tell yourself that everything is okay, you're not in danger. Jot down a few thoughts to remember when panic hits:

Change Your Thoughts

Let's say we have a friend who's obsessing and is extremely worried because her son is overseas in the military—a fairly common concern right now. She could just go about her day, constantly ruminating about his circumstances, endangering her own health, jeopardizing other relationships—and having a miserable time in the process. Or she can take some steps that will enable her to refocus her thoughts and break the fear-worry-stress cycle. Consider these eye-opening insights from Dr. Daniel Amen (*Change Your Brain, Change Your Life*):

> Thoughts are very powerful. They can make your mind and your body feel good, or they can make you feel bad. Every cell in your body is affected by every thought you have. That is why when people get emotionally upset, they frequently develop physical symptoms, such as headaches or stomachaches. Some physicians think that people who have a lot of negative thoughts are more likely to get cancer. If you can think about good things, you will feel better…. You can train your thoughts to be positive and hopeful, or you can allow them to be negative and upset you…. One way to learn how to change your thoughts is to notice them when they are negative and talk back to them. When you just think a negative thought without challenging it, your mind believes it and your body reacts to it. When you correct negative thoughts, you take away their power over you.[8]

So much anxiety in our lives is caused by self-condemning thoughts. Realizing it or not, we wrongfully judge ourselves. A thought enters my mind, I become worried, and then right away I'm thinking, *what's wrong with me?* And then that voice of judgment spirals me downward. "Instead," suggests Nanette, "this should be my reaction: *Oh, I'm worrying again. There's that thing I do.*"

In other words, have a sense of humor as you combat the fear-worry-stress cycle. It really is about choosing; it's about getting to a mental place where you're aware of your thoughts—your meta-cognitions—so you can stop them in their tracks. You *can* shift your thinking to what is far more interesting and even far more peaceful.

MY WORRY-WISE PLAN:
How I Will Change My Thoughts

Sometime this week, use the chart below to document your thoughts, worries, and stressors within a twenty-four-hour cycle. Whenever anxiety strikes—whether mild or severe or in-between—jot down (1) what you're thinking, (2) how you feel, and (3) what struggles are affecting you. Then (below), write what you've observed about yourself during this exercise . . . along with some verses and truths to tell yourself when you feel worried and stressed.

What I've observed about myself when I feel stressed:

Scriptures I will read when I'm anxious and worried:

- 1 Corinthians 13:4–8
- Philippians 4:8
- 1 Peter 5:7
- Additional Passages:

What I'll tell myself when I'm caught up in the fear-worry-stress cycle:

As I unravel wrong thinking, here's how I'll pursue "right talking" (for some clues, read Mark 11:23; Exodus 15:26; Isaiah 53:3–5; Matthew 8:17; 1 Peter 2:24):

24-Hour Cycle	What I'm Thinking When Anxiety Strikes	How I Feel	What I'm Struggling With/ Worried About
Early Morning (Night): 12–3 a.m.			
Early Morning (Night): 3–6 a.m.			
Early Morning (Day): 6–9 a.m.			
Mid- to Late Morning: 9 a.m.–12 p.m.			
Noon Hour: 12–1 p.m.			
Early Afternoon: 1–3 p.m.			
Mid-Afternoon: 3–5 p.m.			
Early Evening: 5–7 p.m.			
Mid-Evening: 7–9 p.m.			
Late Evening: 9 p.m.–12 a.m.			

REFRAME AND REFOCUS

When I (Arnie) begin to feel overwhelmed by my circumstances—especially from worry and stress—I go outside and simply take a walk. As I take in deep breaths of fresh air, I study my environment: the horse arena in the middle of our property, the pastures that surround our house, a pond in the distance. On other occasions, I listen to my favorite tunes as I sweep the stables—anything to put my attention on something different and enjoyable. Very therapeutic, and I've done something productive to boot! My point is this: As negative and worrisome thoughts begin to take over, disconnect them by focusing on your environment. Find something that's not threatening you. Find one thing at a time, and really look hard at it. Then find another thing that's not threatening you. Do this, or these, until you feel better.

MY WORRY-WISE PLAN:
How I Will Refocus

Here are some hands-on, practical things I can do when anxiety strikes:

Tap the Power of the Pen:
Journal Those Nagging Thoughts

Grab a blank notebook or journal and spend fifteen minutes a day acknowledging your worries in a tangible way. Listing your biggest worries and creating a calendar of stressful upcoming activities will enable you to face and deal with each concern so they don't collectively balloon and press you toward panic.

As you write down what you're worried about, include the thoughts and observations you completed above, as well as your imagined worst-case scenarios. In the case of the worried mom, I would encourage her to write a daily letter to her son. Not only will this serve as a release during specific moments, but she also can go back and review what she's written. In the heat of the moment, when anxiety has taken over, you're often not thinking clearly. You may feel as if you're trapped in an all-or-nothing scenario. *I can't take this any longer. It's always going to be this way.* Before you know it, you're overwhelmed within a downward spiral of worry and fear. But if you're not having a full-on panic attack—and if you can journal during those moments—you'll be able to go back and reflect on what you've written.

MY WORRY-WISE PLAN:
How I Can "Journal Away" My Stress

Get started with these simple steps:

(1) First, find a comfy place at a time that's relatively distraction free, if possible, and then begin in prayer. As you talk with God, reflect on the issues in your life that you feel stressed about (again, feel free to use the completed exercises above as a guide).

(2) Do the "look around and find something that's not threatening you" action, if needed. The purpose is to help you step back and more precisely identify sources of stress. When I get worked up, things seem to mush all together and appear to be one massive blob. When I can look at one thing at a time, then I can work on handling one thing at a time. While you're doing this, you might feel upset or angry at first—keep at it until you feel better. Don't run away—take a break, maybe, but come back to it.

(3) Next, write out your worries. Don't waste your time with an "Oh, poor me, how can I possibly handle this" scenario or allow yourself to ruminate on the worries. Stay above that. When you identify something, write it down and move on. Still, please don't rush these steps.

(4) Finally, strive to gain some perspective on your fears, worries, and stresses. Say to yourself, "How is my day today? I was so worried earlier, yet I survived that tough situation. And look at my environment— nothing has changed. I'm okay!" As you do so, you'll eventually have some "aha" moments—those healing points when you're able to view your circumstances through the lens of reality: the what-if thoughts that swirl through our heads are often of our own making and sometimes aren't even real.

Gaining a better perspective enables you to better handle what's worrying you. You just might look at some of these things and realize they're really not problems or worth the stress. And, as you engage these steps, you will definitely be doing something positive to manage stress more effectively.

Get Off Your "Can't" and Take the First Steps Toward Change

In order to reduce worry in your life, change what's within your control. This can involve a range of steps both big and small: For example, consult a debt consolidation service that can help you establish a workable budget; meet with the school's principal about the bullies harassing your daughter; talk to your spouse about moving closer to work so neither one of you is spending half your life stuck in traffic.

Next, look over the worrisome thoughts that you feel you can't take any action on. Consider which are excessive or distorted and have very little basis in reality. Take each of these worrisome thoughts and write down an alternative thought that is more realistic, as a believable challenge to the worry. (See the exercise directly below.) Finally, try to catch yourself when you notice yourself worrying. Stop and tell yourself the alternative thought.

Our Research Says ...

▶ Recording your worries and then reviewing how many really come true can help you appreciate how few, and how relatively rarely, bad things actually do happen.

▶ Relationships can become strained when a spouse (or other loved one) struggles with anxiety. For example, one study found that those suffering with Generalized Anxiety Disorder are twice as likely to have a relationship problem and three times as likely to avoid intimacy with their spouse.

MY WORRY-WISE PLAN:
How I Can Take the First Steps Toward Change

Referring back to your journal, jot down three worries along with three realities and solutions: For example, if you're worried about public speaking, write that in the first column. In the second column, add something that's true about you and your abilities: *I am prepared, I know my material, I will be okay.*

Worries	Realities / Solutions

AT-A-GLANCE STEPS
TO CALMING YOUR MIND

Identify your degree of anxiety as well as worrisome thoughts and what's behind them (insecurity, the constant need for approval, fear of confrontation, etc.).

Discern fearful thoughts that are excessive or distorted and have little basis in reality.

Change what's within your control.

Let go of what's out of your control, and learn to be okay with this.

Catch negative thoughts and replace them with positive ones.

Remind yourself that God is the Shepherd who guides, the One who provides, the Lord of peace during life's trials, the Physician who heals the sick, the Banner that guides the soldier. "Be still, and know that I am God."[9]

Accept yourself as you are, knowing that it's perfectly acceptable to perform at your own level instead of at someone—anyone—else's.

Face tasks that push you out of your comfort zone, but release those that are distractions or that just aren't necessary.

De-shame the fear of failing, of being blamed for something, of making a mistake, of having a life-controlling struggle, etc.

De-clutter by reducing busy schedules and striving to simplify life.

Recap and Reflect
Talking Points for Couples or Group Study

- ⟩ We can break the fear-worry-stress cycle by attaining homeostasis—balance between stimulating and tranquilizing chemical forces in our bodies.

  - ✳ *How will I work toward accomplishing this in our home?*

- ⟩ Identify the worries that are plaguing your family (your spouse and kids) and you, and plot a course of action:

  My wife / husband / child, _____, often frets about:

  Next, write a message your spouse or child may need to hear repeatedly:

1) An encouraging phrase that will help your loved one dispute a false thought or irrational fear: "Tell yourself this Chinese proverb: 'Tension is who you think you should be. Relaxation is who you are.'[10] EVERYTHING will be okay. YOU will be okay."

2) A Bible verse: "So do not be afraid. I am with you. Do not be terrified. I am your God. I will make you strong and help you. My powerful right hand will take good care of you. I always do what is right." (Isaiah 41:10 NIRV).

3) A reminder about how much we are loved and valued by God: "We can trust the Lord. He has not abandoned us; he is with us and loves us more than we can ever imagine."

Here's what I will communicate as often as needed:

(Repeat this process for yourself.)

▶ Here are some negative behaviors that my family and I will work toward changing and some positive ones we can start doing:

Change:

Do:

Change:

Do:

Chapter Four

THE SECRET OF HEALTHY LIVING
(De-Stressing Our Body)

We must be blunt about a serious matter: Inactivity and stress are a deadly mix. If our body is constantly overloaded with adrenaline, yet we're not working off the nervous energy, then we're putting so much stress on our heart and other vital organs. And the worst thing we can do is fill an inactive, anxious body with depressants, stimulants, and fat: sugary or caffeinated drinks, fried foods and desserts, salty canned or prepared foods, nicotine, alcohol…

On the positive side: Exercise is a powerful stress reducer, and our age or inexperience shouldn't hold us back. Everyone *can* take steps to improve his/her physical condition. What's more, getting active will benefit our mood and help us to be happier, healthier Christ-followers!

Of course, we must be smart and start out slowly, gradually increasing the amount and intensity of our workouts. Once we have combined exercise with a balanced diet, we'll be well on our way toward a worry-free lifestyle. The fact is, stress and worrying provoke some people to eat too little, others too much, or to eat unhealthy foods. Keep your health in mind whenever worrying nudges you toward the fridge.

YOUR BODY'S WORRY-WISE PLAN

Ready to continue building the new you? Begin by talking with your primary care physician. Get a thorough physical exam to make sure other health problems are not fueling your feelings of anxiety. Your doctor may prescribe medication such as anti-anxiety drugs or antidepressants to help you self-manage anxiety and excessive worry.

Once you get the green light, try the following.

Stretch and Relax

My (Michael's) wife, Tiffany, incorporates a variety of stretching routines into her daily exercise regimen. For example, she does stretches for her back, for her legs, feet, and ankles, and for her shoulders and arms. Tiffany often ties in a spiritual element with each maneuver: she meditates on Scripture, and she prays to Jesus during her workouts. Her focus is on relaxing through proper stretching and breathing and also endeavoring to set her mind on God's peace.

"[Stretching] is peaceful, relaxing, and noncompetitive," writes fitness expert Bob Anderson in *Stretching*.[1] "The subtle, invigorating feelings of stretching allow you to get in touch with your muscles.… It relaxes your mind and tunes up your body, and it should be part of your daily life." (Tiffany highly recommends his excellent book.)

Breathe Deep

When that pang of anxiety strikes and your heart begins to race, take a simple step that can help quiet your mind and calm your emotions and body. Breathe in slowly to the count of six, then breathe out slowly to the count of six. Do this for five minutes; gradually increase to twenty minutes over time. The point is to slow your heart rate and reduce the pace at which stress hormones are flying through your system. While focusing on each breath, remind yourself that the anxiety you're feeling is a chemical response.[2] Repeat some phrases, verses, or prayers: "Relax and live in truth, not fear"; "Be at rest; know that God is in control"; "Lord Jesus, calm my mind and my body. Please give me peace."

Deep breathing is helpful in interrupting irrational thoughts. But the key is to take long, steady breaths from the diaphragm. This slows down your heart rate, lowers blood pressure, and helps your body use oxygen more efficiently. It also has a calming effect. Our lungs supply red blood cells with fresh oxygen—enabling normal cell function and proper metabolism—and they also rid our bodies of harmful waste products like carbon dioxide.

Exercise Daily

God designed our body to be active. The harder we work it, and the better the nutrients we put into it, the leaner, stronger, and more energetic it will become. In fact, the chemicals produced during moderate exercise can enhance the function of the immune system and train our bodies to deal with stress under controlled circumstances.

Here are the two types of exercise we need to incorporate into our daily lives:

Aerobic Activity. The technical definition is "training with oxygen." In other words, an activity that gets your heart pumping and air flowing through your body: walking, hiking, jogging, swimming, bicycling, cross-country skiing. The benefits are indisputable:

▶ Our heart is strengthened
▶ Blood pressure is lowered
▶ Metabolism is improved
▶ Fat stores are burned after twenty to thirty minutes of sustained activity
▶ Endorphins and other "feel good" hormones are released

Anaerobic Exercise. This means "training without oxygen," and it involves all forms of high-intensity activity engaged for short periods of time. Examples include sprinting, resistance training (working out with weights), powerlifting, tennis, racquetball, and any other sport you can think of that causes fatigue to the muscles with harder but shorter bursts of energy. During anaerobic exercise, our cardiovascular system has a challenging time delivering the necessary levels of oxygen to our muscles fast enough. And since muscles require air to maintain prolonged exertion, anaerobic exercises can only continue for brief stretches. Why is this important for overall good health? Resistance training provides benefits like these:

▶ Improves muscle strength, which enhances other athletic pursuits
▶ Builds and maintains a lean, toned body
▶ Enhances weight loss
▶ Fights stress through vigorous exercise

CHECKLIST OF
FAMILY-FRIENDLY EXERCISES

☐ Take a twenty-minute walk each evening around your neighborhood

☐ Go for a Saturday-morning bike ride

☐ Play "adults vs. kids" football or soccer in the backyard

☐ Engage in a once-a-week hike at a local park, the mountains, the beach

☐ Swim and work out at the YMCA (or other family-oriented health club)

☐ Take a karate class together

☐ Get up early three days a week and stretch together—followed by family devotions

☐ Host a laser tag or paintball marathon

☐ Pop an aerobic-style game into the Wii or Xbox and work out together

☐ Jog three nights a week at a local park or on an indoor track

MY WORRY-WISE PLAN:
Weekly Stretching, Deep Breathing, and Exercise Routine

DAY	AEROBIC AND ANAEROBIC EXERCISE	STRETCHING & BREATHING
Sunday	:	
Monday	:	
Tuesday	:	
Wednesday	:	
Thursday	:	
Friday	:	
Saturday	:	

MY FITNESS GOALS	FITNESS GOALS FOR MY FAMILY

Know That Eating Smart Can Promote Worry-Free Living

A well-balanced diet is crucial to good health and will enable you to reduce the fear-worry-stress cycle. Certain foods and drinks can stimulate our bodies and actually trigger anxiety. In other words, that daily run to your favorite coffee spot is a fun vice, but in the long run it might be taking a toll on your health: Think about the caffeine, sugar, and fat you put into your body. Think about how you feel after your body crashes. More stressed—right?

Here are some dietary steps that we guarantee will reap profound benefits:

Cut Back on Caffeine. You're probably getting more of this than you think, especially if you consume daily doses of coffee, tea, chocolate, energy drinks, and many soft drinks.

What happens inside our body: Caffeine stimulates the nervous system, which—as you know—triggers the release of adrenaline, making you feel nervous and jittery. Some medical professionals claim there is a link between caffeine intake and high blood pressure as well as high cholesterol levels.[3]

Our advice: Consume caffeinated beverages in moderation. For example, no more than two cups of coffee in the morning. This will provide more than enough caffeine to increase your alertness and increase activity in your muscles, nervous system, and heart. In excess, caffeine can increase our stress levels.

Limit or Eliminate Alcohol. It's ironic, really. Some people drink beer or wine to calm their nerves. But in reality, large amounts of alcohol make us feel more stressed out.

What happens inside our body: Alcohol stimulates the secretion of adrenaline, which affects nervous tension. The result: When the buzz wears off, we end up feeling irritable, and we may even struggle to fall asleep. Excess alcohol can increase fat deposits in the heart, decrease immune function, and limit the liver's ability to remove toxins from the body.

Our advice: A glass or two of red wine with a meal can be very useful and has even been shown to benefit the cardiovascular system. But use common sense: alcohol is addictive and can be easily abused. Moderation is the key.

Reduce Sugar Intake. Our craving for sweets starts at an early age. Yet sugar has no essential nutrients. It gives us a quick boost of energy, and then we crash.

What happens inside our body: Our adrenal glands become exhausted—i.e., the crash—and we begin feeling irritable and have difficulty concentrating. We may even feel depressed. In addition, much sugar is bad for the pancreas and increases the possibility of developing diabetes.

Our advice: Keep your blood sugar constant, and never use sugar as a pick-me-up.

Use Salt Sparingly. We need salt (or sodium chloride) to help our bodies function properly, but most of us are getting way too much of it. Check the labels of processed foods, and you'll probably find sodium chloride in the list of ingredients. Order a meal from your favorite restaurant, and more than likely you'll be served a dish that's high in sodium. According to the Mayo Clinic, the average American should limit salt to less than 2,300 milligrams a day—or 1,500 if you're fifty-one or older and/or have high blood pressure, diabetes, or chronic kidney disease. Most of us consume more than 3,400 milligrams of salt per day.[4]

What happens inside our body: Sodium chloride aids nutrient absorption and transport, and when salt breaks down into its two chemical components, chloride becomes part of the acids in our digestive tract. These absorb nutrients from our food. Sodium, the other component, influences the volume of liquids retained by our body outside of our cells.[5] This determines our blood volume, which in turn regulates blood pressure. In excess, however, it can deplete adrenal glands and cause emotional instability. Even worse, it can increase our blood pressure and can put us at risk for heart disease.

Our advice: While salt plays an important role in our body's proper functioning, we must use it sparingly. Consider a salt substitute that has potassium rather than sodium. Avoid junk foods (e.g., potato chips) and foods cured with salt (e.g., bacon and ham); cease using table salt.

Cut Back on Fatty Foods. According to medical professionals, there are three main types of dietary fats: unsaturated fats (which include monounsaturated and polyunsaturated fats), saturated fats, and trans fats. Most of us are all too familiar with the immediate effect of fatty foods—tummy discomfort, gas, bloating, acid reflux, and heartburn. But somehow we overlook the most lethal risk: heart disease. Some fats are necessary for wellness, but others should be limited or avoided as much as possible. Let's take a closer look at the good, the bad, and the ugly risks associated with a diet high in fat.

What happens inside our body: Monounsaturated and polyunsaturated are the good fats that actually improve cholesterol levels and decrease our risk for cardiovascular disease. These fats are found in nuts, avocados, and olive oil. Polyunsaturated fats include omega-3 and omega-6 fatty acids, essential to our body's needs. Saturated fat is primarily found in animal products, such as meat and dairy products, as well as in coconut and palm oils. This fat type is unhealthy and may increase our risk of type 2 (adult-onset) diabetes as well as heart disease by increasing our LDL ("bad") cholesterol. Trans fat (the most unhealthy kind) is a major enemy to our body; it can increase our LDL cholesterol and decrease our HDL ("good") cholesterol, increase our risk of cardiovascular disease and type 2 diabetes, and lead to insulin resistance.

Our advice: Avoid eating foods full of saturated fats. As fat accumulates in our body, we end up gaining weight and risk becoming obese. An unhealthy weight gain can lead to chronic illnesses like diabetes, heart disease, and arthritis. It also adds unnecessary stress on the cardiovascular system and puts us at a greater risk for a heart attack. In addition, a high-fat diet is believed to cause breast, colon, and prostate cancers.

FOODS TO EAT

▸ *Healthy Carbs* (also known as good carbohydrates): Whole grains such as whole wheat, brown rice, millet, quinoa, and barley; beans, fruits, and vegetables. Whole grains help the brain produce serotonin, which increases our sense of well-being.

▸ *Green, Yellow, and Orange Vegetables:* These are all rich in minerals, vitamins, and phytochemicals, which boost immune response and protect against disease. Eating more vegetables can increase our brain's serotonin production. Also, vegetables contain the natural, safe form of L-tryptophan.

▸ *Seafood:* Foods from the ocean are high in selenium, and, according to Dr. Reginald B. Cherry, "Studies have determined that people who do not get enough selenium tend to suffer more depression, fatigue, and even anxiety. When enough selenium is available, mood changes improve significantly."[6] David Zinczenko, author of the popular book series *Eat This, Not That*, recommends these fish choices: Wild Alaskan salmon, farmed rainbow trout, Pacific halibut, farmed catfish, farmed tilapia, yellowfin tuna, mahi-mahi.[7]

▸ *Flavonoids and Resveratrol:* These can be found in grapes—specifically in red wine. Flavonoids have been effective in fighting diseases ranging from cancer to heart disease to circulatory problems. Resveratrol inhibits tumor growth at three different stages: initiation, promotion, and progression. Both are available in supplements as well as in certain juices and teas.

FOODS TO AVOID

▶ *Fried Foods:* Steer clear of foods rich in fat. These are immune depressing, especially when stress is taking its toll on our bodies.

▶ *Unhealthy Carbs:* These are foods like white flour, refined sugar, and white rice, which have been stripped of all bran, fiber, and nutrients. Unhealthy carbs digest quickly and cause spikes in blood sugar levels and energy.[8]

▶ *Foods High in Sugar:* According to *Men's Health,* the average American is consuming 460 calories from added sugars every day—more than 100 pounds of raw sugar per person per year (enough to make 3,628 Reese's Peanut Butter Cups).[9] All this sugar excess is leading to an epidemic of obesity and other illnesses, including type 2 diabetes and cancer. So as you make your way through the supermarket, check labels closely. Sugar is often defined as monosaccharides (galactose, glucose, fructose) and disaccharides (sucrose, lactose, maltose). All such foods should be limited or avoided.

MY WORRY-WISE PLAN:
Weekly Menu and Dietary Goals for My Family and Me

DAY	WEEKLY MENU	PORTIONS (AND CALORIES PER SERVING)
Sunday	*Fruits:* *Vegetables:* *Whole Grains:* *Healthy Protein:*	
Monday	*Fruits:* *Vegetables:* *Whole Grains:* *Healthy Protein:*	
Tuesday	*Fruits:* *Vegetables:* *Whole Grains:* *Healthy Protein:*	
Wednesday	*Fruits:* *Vegetables:* *Whole Grains:* *Healthy Protein:*	
Thursday	*Fruits:* *Vegetables:* *Whole Grains:* *Healthy Protein:*	
Friday	*Fruits:* *Vegetables:* *Whole Grains:* *Healthy Protein:*	
Saturday	*Fruits:* *Vegetables:* *Whole Grains:* *Healthy Protein:*	

MY NUTRITIONAL GOALS	NUTRITIONAL GOALS FOR MY FAMILY	FOODS & BEVERAGES TO LIMIT OR AVOID

AT-A-GLANCE STEPS
TO CALMING YOUR BODY

Exercise weekly at least, daily if possible. Without question, the chemicals produced during moderate exercise can enhance the function of the immune system as well as train your body to deal with stress.

Breathe slowly to the count of six, and then breathe out slowly to the count of six. Do this for five minutes; gradually increase to twenty minutes over time.

Stretch to keep your muscles supple, to make your body feel more relaxed, to prepare you for motion, and to help you stay fit.

Eat a healthy, balanced diet. Stress and worry provoke some people to skip meals or to eat too little and others to consume too much and/or to attach to unhealthy foods.

Drink an appropriate amount of water every day. This flushes toxins from vital organs and carries nutrients to your cells. How much? That depends on your health, how active you are, and where you live.

Engage in relaxing and enjoyable hobbies.

Connect with family and friends every day.

Laugh! It lifts your spirits, especially if you feel run-down. It's a good idea to avoid taking yourself too seriously and to laugh at your shortcomings.

Savor a moment with your spouse, a walk in the park, a piece of art, a song, time spent outdoors, etc. What's more, getting sunshine and fresh air daily can be good for your emotions and your overall health.

Detox by avoiding or limiting substances such as caffeine, nicotine, and alcohol.

Sleep seven to nine hours every day if you're an adult; teens and kids need more. Lack of sleep can inhibit productivity, trigger anxiety, and lead to serious health consequences.

Recap and Reflect
Talking Points for Couples or Group Study

▶ List some key ways that you will strive to improve the overall health of your family.

Diet:

Exercise:

Healthcare Visits:

Ways to Relax:

Family Connections:

Sleep:

❋ What healthy steps do you plan to take in the days and weeks ahead?

▶ Clue in to your family's communication style. This is a crucial step in order to help—not push away—a loved one. Ask yourself this: What kinds of conversations, words, or phrases cause walls to go up between my family and me? (How can I avoid these things—and work on tearing down existing walls?) How can I improve communication with my family?

Chapter Five

THE SECRET OF
CHRIST-CENTERED GROWTH
(Transforming Our Spirit)

*Loving God with all our heart, soul, and mind
(Matthew 22:37).*

*Engaging the Bible—and having a two-way connection
with Jesus.*

Pondering God's Word deep in our heart.

These are the basics of the Christian faith—activities that
should be second nature to every Christ-follower, right? Yet
somewhere along the way, every believer can get off track spiritually. As we mentioned in chapter 2 (and will explore more
deeply in the next chapter), Christians are busy people.

In fact, we're busy *being busy*: soccer practice twice a week,
that big meeting on Monday, choir practice on Wednesday, date
night on Friday, grocery shopping, bills to pay, vacations to plan,
meals to make, e-mails to send … *busy, busy, busy.*

And instead of having a thriving relationship with Jesus, we risk settling for a "god of rules." Basically, there are two types of Christians:

Notional Christ-followers: those who believe in "their concept" of Christ and interact with Him in a one-way relationship. In other words, a notional believer communicates to a concept of Christ in their mind as opposed to experiencing a two-way relationship with the true Christ. There are no significant behavioral differences between the notional believer and an individual who claims not to follow Christ at all.

Relational Christ-followers: those who have a two-way relationship with the one true Christ of the Bible. These individuals have a relationship with Jesus Christ through a saving faith based on the Word of God. This two-way relationship is initiated when we come to grips with our sin, we recognize our need for a Savior, and we receive Jesus Christ into our lives as our only Savior from sin. This relationship begins when the Holy Spirit places the new believer into the Body of Christ and begins a two-way relationship fostered by prayer (talking to) and personally engaging Scripture (hearing from God) on a regular basis. This kind of faith, if genuine, produces measurable behavioral results that are reflected in lifestyle choices and differences that make the relational Christ-follower distinct both from the notional one and from those who don't claim to follow Christ at all.

We've learned through the years that we have to give up our notions about Jesus and begin pursuing the one true God of the Bible. Everyone seeks intimacy with God, whether or not they're willing to admit it. Ignore this need, and you end up looking for him in the wrong places. It's sort of like drinking sand because you believe it is an oasis, but it's only a mirage.

God designed us to bond relationally with himself. As author Doug Banister points out, "All of us are on a lifelong quest to know Him more intimately. We must learn how to bond with Him if we are to become the people He has called us to be. The cost of failing to bond with God can be staggering: addiction, low self-confidence, depression, religiosity, burnout, and relational problems." [1]

The God of the Bible is a relational God. The three members of the Trinity—God the Father, God the Son, and God the Spirit—exist in relationship together. Jesus describes their relationship as intensely intimate. Jesus says to the Father, "You are in me and I am in you" (John 17:21).

As Banister points out, the creation story is an account of a relational God creating a man and a woman he could bond, revealing to us and through us the unity of the Godhead. We find a clue about the heart of God when we read, "Let us make mankind in our image, in our likeness" (Genesis 1:26). God, who exists in relationship, creates men and women who bear this same relational likeness.[2]

God did not create just one human being, but two. When Adam was the only person in the universe, God said, "It is not good for the man to be alone" (Genesis 2:18). Why isn't it? Was relationship with God not enough for him? Evidently not. Adam needed to be in relationship with God and in relationship with other people. This is why Jesus summed up all the teaching of Scripture in two simple commands: love God and love your neighbor. The *r* word, "relationship," is what the Good News is all about … restoring the relationship for which our Father originally created us.

"Relationship, or bonding, then, is at the foundation of God's nature," writes Christian psychologist Henry Cloud. "Since we are created in His likeness, relationship is our most fundamental need, the very foundation of who we are. Without relationship, without attachment to God and others, we can't be our true selves. We can't be truly human."[3]

LUKEWARM FAITH ISN'T REALLY FAITH AT ALL

Considering the importance of a thriving relationship that develops over time, and understanding that religious rituals and practices can't save us, we have been wrestling with some difficult questions about what makes someone a sincere Christian.

Think about this: Are we mistaken and even misled in counting people saved who have not allowed their relationship to take hold and grow? And what about someone who has never experienced meaningful changes in his or her life?

Say, for example, a man commits his heart to Christ and yet continues in a sexual relationship with a woman he isn't married to (we know what the Bible says about sexual sin). And what if this same man hasn't demonstrated any changes in his life? He doesn't pray or read his Bible; he doesn't attend church. What if, after praying that prayer of salvation, he hasn't really done anything to grow closer to Christ? Perhaps his life is the same as it was before.

Is he really a Christian?

These are questions that the church has been debating for

centuries. So, perhaps, the answers depend upon your theology. Thankfully, though, God is the final judge—not us. He knows who is sincere in their faith. Yet in our professions, we have worked with some desperate people (both inside and outside the church). And we've witnessed real victory over addiction and sin. Through it all, the words of 2 Corinthians 5:17 ring loudly in our ears: "If anyone is in Christ, he is a new creation; old things have passed away; behold, all things have become new" (NKJV).

And four other words scream through our brains as well: "I never knew you."

These are painful words to us—maybe the most terrifying in the Bible. Jesus spoke them while teaching on a mountainside: "Not everyone who says to me, 'Lord, Lord,' will enter the kingdom of heaven, but only he who does the will of my Father who is in heaven. Many will say to me on that day, 'Lord, Lord, did we not prophesy in your name, and in your name drive out demons and perform many miracles?' Then I will tell them plainly, I never knew you. Away from me, you evildoers!'" (Matthew 7:21–23).

Does this include Christ-followers too?

We know Jesus was warning about religious phonies and people he described a few verses earlier as "ferocious wolves" in sheep's clothing. But what about ordinary Christian folks who mess up from time to time?

What about the times when we doubt … or the seasons when we don't feel close to God? What about the struggles we often battle?

Is Jesus saying that it's all about a perfect score? If we don't always do the dos and avoid the don'ts, is it possible that we could miss eternity too?

Is God that cruel?

The answer to these questions, of course, is NO! God loves us passionately despite our imperfections. Change does not bring about salvation. Instead, salvation produces change in our lives. And God is incredibly patient as he works it all out step-by-step.

Yet here's something that troubles us: too often when new believers exhibit no change in their lifestyles or when they revert to former lifestyles, we refer to them as "unsanctified carnal Christians." However, based on our research—not theology—the term *carnal Christian* appears to be useless with regard to discipleship and genuine faith.

From a scientific standpoint, confirmed by both Barna and Gallup, if there is no behavior that separates the carnal Christian from the non-Christian, there is really no such thing as a carnal Christian. These are simply people who made a profession of faith but are yet in their sins. Again, only God can judge the heart; research cannot. But research analyzes behaviors … and where there are no changed behaviors from notional Christ-followers, there is reason to suspect the genuineness of their salvation.

Here's what Jesus said: "Do men gather grapes from thorn bushes or figs from thistles? Even so, every good tree bears good fruit, but a bad tree bears bad fruit. Therefore by their fruits you will know them" (Matthew 7:16–17, 20 NKJV).

The test of true life in Christ is growth and maturation, not verbal profession.

We have observed significant behavioral and lifestyle differences between Christ-followers who know what the Bible is and what it is for and those who don't.

Engaging God's Word really works!

With that said, are you ready to stop searching in the dark? Are you yearning to fall in love with Jesus and to begin pursuing him with all your heart?

Are you ready to take the next step in breaking the fear-worry-stress cycle?

YOUR SPIRIT'S WORRY-WISE PLAN

Prayer, praise, and meditation on God's Word are three basic disciplines that can have a profound impact on every believer's life. We have observed that people of faith are better able to handle the stressors of life if they're practicing their faith. So to have that spiritual connection and to take it a step further is pragmatically utilizing your faith in daily life. This could mean ten to fifteen minutes of prayer and meditation. Not only will this help you in the moment and throughout the day, but this kind of spiritual practice will have a physiological cumulative effect on your life, one that will help you deal with the fear-worry-stress cycle.

Prayer

Instead of worrying over our problems, which simply fuels anxiety and stress, God's Word recommends taking everything to him in prayer. Paul's letter to the Philippians (the first two chapters, specifically) reveals that as we pray, our minds will be protected by a peace that goes beyond our ability to understand.

Through prayer, we can open a window that allows God's eternal love and healing power to shine into our lives; we can open our hands to receive his many blessings; we can open our hearts to let his presence fill and strengthen us.

In the words of R. C. Sproul,

> The Lord God of the universe, the Creator and Sustainer of all things … not only commands us to pray, but also invites us to make our requests known…. In the act and dynamic of praying, I bring my whole life under His gaze. Yes, He knows what is in my mind, but I still have the privilege of articulating to Him what is there. He says, "Come. Speak to Me. Make your requests known to Me." And so, we come in order to know Him and to be known by Him.[4]

God hears and answers our prayers. But we must be proactive. We must open the window by kneeling before him in prayer. Jesus says that we have not because we ask not. James tells us a righteous person's effectual, fervent prayer accomplishes much. Again and again, God's holy Word reveals to us that prayer is an effective tool. That is, prayer works.

God delights in our prayers. He longs to demonstrate his power in the tremendous trials that shake the foundation of our lives as well as in the tiny troubles that annoy us. Giant needs are never too great for his power; small ones are never too insignificant for his love.

God answers prayer because he is the supreme ruler of all. He governs both world events and our individual lives, ready at our request to act, to intervene, to overrule for our good, for his glory, and for the progress of the gospel.

God moves through prayer. Not only are we called to this activity,[5] we're also assured of God's action in response. As his Word clearly states, God promises results if we pray. [6] He has assured us that prayer is the way to secure his aid and move his mighty hand. Even in sickness, failure, rejection, or financial distress, we can pray and experience his peace.

> "Have faith in God, Jesus answered. "I tell you the truth, if anyone says to this mountain, 'Go, throw yourself into the sea,' and does not doubt in his heart but believes that what he says will happen, it will be done for him."[7]

Our Lord Jesus often slipped away to be alone and to pray. Margaret Magdalen wrote:

> Jesus needed the silence of eternity as a thirsting man in the desert needs water…. He longed for time apart to bask and sunbathe in His Father's love, to soak in it and repose in it. No matter how drained He felt, it seems that this deep, silent communion refreshed Him more than a good night's sleep.[8]

Meditation on the Word of God

If I'm so busy being worried all the time, then my heart isn't focused on God's Word. The Bible is filled with incredible promises from him. Meditating on these words of assurance can dispel our worry, doubt, anxiety, fear, and stress.[9] Here are just three more examples:

> The Lord will keep you safe from secret traps and deadly diseases. He will spread his wings over you and keep you secure. His faithfulness is like a shield or a city wall. You won't need to worry about dangers at night or arrows during the day. And you won't fear diseases that strike in the dark or sudden disaster at noon.[10]

> Be anxious for nothing, but in everything by prayer and supplication, with thanksgiving, let your requests be made known to God; and the peace of God, which surpasses all understanding, will guard your hearts and minds through Christ Jesus.[11]

> Let the peace of Christ keep you in tune with each other, in step with each other. None of this going off and doing your own thing. And cultivate thankfulness. Let the Word of Christ—the Message—have the run of the house. Give it plenty of room in your lives. Instruct and direct one another using good common sense. And sing, sing your hearts out to God! Let every detail in your lives—words, actions, whatever—be done in the name of the Master, Jesus, thanking God the Father every step of the way.[12]

Praise and Worship

Someone once said: "I find it to be almost impossible to be stressed and praise God at the same time. When I'm anxious, I just start praising and the worry just seems to go away."[13]

Wise advice.

Praising and worshiping God is an interactive experience. It's both private and public. It involves our heart and our head. And, as we linger in God's presence, praising him, we connect with the divine—the very Source of life. "Come near to God and he will come near to you."[14]

Praise is the spontaneous response of a grateful child of God in his presence. That's how Henry Blackaby describes it.

> The person who knows God and experiences Him intimately sings to the Lord with deepest praise! Mary was overwhelmed by the Lord's goodness to her. In response, she sang one of the most beautiful and profound songs of praise found in Scripture. Trying to stop the praise of a thankful heart would be like trying to arrest the flow of a mighty waterfall! God created us to praise Him; praise will be our activity when we are gathered around His throne in heaven.[15]

MY WORRY-WISE PLAN:
Steps Toward Peace

Study John 14 and 16.

Jesus tells us, "Do not let your hearts be troubled. Believe in God, believe also in me."[16] He also says, "If you love me, you will keep my commandments. And I will ask the Father, and he will give you another Advocate, to be with you forever. This is the Spirit of truth."[17] And, "When the Spirit of truth comes, he will guide you into all the truth."[18]

Why are these messages from Jesus crucial to combating anxiety and overcoming worry?

Share how you believe God's truth will deliver you and your family from worry.

Memorize Scriptures that emphasize God's power, protection, and provision.

Here's one to consider:

> Humble yourselves therefore under the mighty hand of God, so that he may exalt you in due time. Cast all your anxiety on him, because he cares for you. Discipline yourselves, keep alert. Like a roaring lion your adversary the devil prowls around, looking for someone to devour. Resist him, steadfast in your faith, for you know that your brothers and sisters in all the world are undergoing the same kinds of suffering. And after you have suffered for a little while, the God of all grace, who has called you to his eternal glory in Christ, will himself restore, support, strengthen, and establish you (1 Peter 5:6–10 NRSV).

Make a list of twelve verses/passages you plan to memorize during the next year.

1.

2.

3.

4.

5.

6.

7.

8.

9.

10.

11.

12.

Pray for release from the weight of worry—and trust that God *will* answer you!

Reflect on these prayers:

Cleanse our mind, O Lord we beseech thee, of all anxious thoughts for ourselves, that we may learn not to trust in the abundance of what we have, save as tokens of thy goodness and grace, but that we may commit ourselves in faith to thy keeping, and devote all our energy of soul, mind, and body to the work of thy kingdom and the furthering of the purposes of thy divine righteousness; through Jesus Christ our Lord.[19]

—*Euchologium Anglicanum*

Strengthen me, O God, by the grace of Thy Holy Spirit; grant me to be strengthened with might in the inner man, and to put away from my heart all useless anxiety and distress, and let me never be drawn aside by various longings after anything whatever, whether it be worthless or precious; but may I regard all things as passing away, and myself as passing away with them. For nothing is lasting under the sun, for all things are vanity and vexation of spirit. Oh, how wise is he who thus regards them.[20]

—*Thomas à Kempis*

Share what you see to be the common spiritual thread woven into these two prayers.

How would you pray in this same vein? Write your prayer in any words you choose.

For help with standing against fear and worry, consider starting either an accountability group or an accountability relationship with one other person.

Which people would I like to talk with about this?

How often would I prefer to meet?

What would be my expectations?

Tonight, and again anytime, consider expressing this prayer by Dietrich Bonhoeffer:

O Lord my God, I thank you that you have brought this day to a close;
I thank you that you have given me peace in body and soul.
Your hand has been over me and has protected and preserved me.
Forgive my puny faith, the ill that I this day have done,
and help me to forgive all who have wronged me.
Grant me a quiet night's sleep beneath your tender care.
And defend me from all the temptations of darkness.
Into your hands I commend my loved ones
And all who dwell in this house;
I commend my body and soul.
O God, your holy name be praised. Amen.[21]

Our Research Says . . .

▶ Couples who pray and read the Bible together at home enjoy higher levels of satisfaction in their marriage. Moreover, a strong spiritual bond helps to buffer the stresses of life.

▶ If you struggle with worry and anxiety, you're in renowned company. Abraham Lincoln, Barbara Bush, John Steinbeck, Charles Schultz, Sir Isaac Newton, and Oprah Winfrey, for example, have had to deal with one or more conditions known as an anxiety disorder.[28]

AT-A-GLANCE STEPS
TO CALMING YOUR SPIRIT

Confess to Jesus everything that's bottled up inside: sins, mistakes, fears, worries, disappointments … absolutely *everything!*

Talk to Jesus during uninterrupted prayer times and continually throughout the day, especially during stressful moments. "No one can pray and worry at the same time."[22]

Praise! Express your love to Jesus as you give him your worship and your heart.

Receive God's Word into your mind by reading, listening to, and "spiritually consuming" the words of the Bible. Consistently be asking, *what does God say about giving up control and surrendering everything to Him?*

Reflect actively, on God's Word, thinking, meditating, and pondering the message of the Bible into your heart. *How can surrendering my life bring more peace into each day?*

Respond to God's Word, looking for ways to live out the truth. *What are some steps I've decided I will take in order to let go of worry?*

Worship, remembering that this is to be an interactive experience.[23] *When we're close to Jesus, praising and worshiping him, what happens to worry?*

Rest in his promises, in his protection, in his love. "There is no fear in love. But perfect love drives out fear, because fear has to do with punishment. The one who fears is not made perfect in love."[24]

Trust, for no one whose hope is in God will ever be put to shame.[25] "Worry does not empty tomorrow of its sorrow. It empties today of its strength."[26]

Go and face tomorrow, because he is constantly at our side, loving us and encouraging us. When we hurt, God hurts. And we're to do the same for our friends.[27]

Recap and Reflect
Talking Points for Couples or Group Study

▶ The Worry-Wise Plan is a mind-body-spirit solution that helps people unravel wrong thinking and negative thoughts. Consider again these words: "Don't copy the behavior and customs of this world, but let God transform you into a new person by changing the way you think. Then you will learn to know God's will for you, which is good and pleasing and perfect."[29]

  ✻ *Do I and my family fit right in with the world's ways, or are we becoming new people as we learn to change our thinking and as those thoughts become our choices and actions?* Explain.

▶ Consider how you and your family can turn to God when troubles hit—and avoid spiraling into the fear-worry-stress cycle. Begin by taking to heart this passage of Scripture: "Peace I leave with you; my peace I give you. I do not give to you as the world gives. Do not let your hearts be troubled and do not be afraid" (John 14:27).

Here's how I will try to model these verses:

Here are some biblical lessons that I will share with my loved ones:

Here are some practical steps my family can take that will help build our trust in God and decrease stress in our home:

▶ Managing worry can be lasting and successful when we learn to let go of yesterday's troubles and stop ruminating about tomorrow. We are to find peace with God today … in this moment.

❋ *Do I believe this? Why or why not?*

Chapter Six

THE SECRET OF BALANCE

Rough water ahead—paddle left!" Jeffery shouts to fifteen-year-old Jonathan.

"No, Dad, let's go left, so paddle right."

"Son, listen to me," Jeffery says, sternly. "There are big rocks and strong rapids on the left. We need to veer right. Quickly!"

Jonathan points downstream. "But do you see that?" he asks. "There's junk in the water. Maybe it's a fallen tree or something."

"We'll take our chances," Jeffery responds, digging his paddle in and stroking harder. "We'll flip if we hit the rapids."

"But, Dad—"

"Don't argue. Paddle left. *Now!*"

In just another instant, *THUMP! BUMP!* The canoe strikes a mound of twisted branches clogging a narrow strip of Colorado's Gunnison River. The vessel begins to rock violently but doesn't tip over. Seconds later the water is calm again.

Jonathan turns around and grins. "Okay, you were right—this time!"

Jeffery high-fives his son, then slumps back in the canoe. "I think we're getting the hang of this adventure thing," he says. "Now if we could just figure out some challenges back home."

THE TWISTS AND TURNS OF FAMILY LIFE

Hurried, hassled home lives. Overextended schedules. Days, weeks, and months—hours, minutes, and seconds—all set on fast-forward.

Navigating life can seem very much like a perpetual ride over wild and torrential rapids. Our safe passage depends upon our faith in God, the strength of our connections with loved ones, our physical, mental, and emotional health … and how we manage stress.

During my (so far) twenty-seven-year ministry to teens and their families, I've found that life-changing lessons are best learned experientially—especially when they're taught with the great outdoors as a backdrop. A few years ago, Jeffery, Jonathan, and a dozen other father-son pairs—including me (Michael) and my son, Christopher—took a four-day adventure through Colorado's canyon country. In the end, we had faced the rapids head-on, and we'd come away stronger. Our mission that week was to break through barriers that tear families apart.

It takes cooperation and communication to keep canoes stable, making them ideal vessels for bringing families together in shared adventure and toward deepened relationships. Even so, the most powerful moments happened back on shore. Each evening the men and boys gathered around a campfire, discussing the lessons they'd learned on the river. Inevitably, they pulled off their masks and shared what was inside.

"I'm so proud of you, Jonathan, for trusting me today," Jeffery told his son one night. "We were a solid team, which is how God wants us to be."

Jonathan smiled and put his arm around his father. "My heart was racing, and I felt so scared when I saw the rapids," he said. "But you stayed calm. That really helped. And when we came through okay, it gave me more confidence."

The teen paused, thought carefully about his words, and then continued. "I wish it could be this way at home. It's like, there's so much stress. Your job; Mom saying we have more bills than money; pressure at school; the way we fight sometimes. Maybe we can start handling troubles like we did today."

Another father, Paul, vowed to spend more time with his seventeen-year-old son David. "We get busy, with each of us moving fast and in so many different directions," he said. "We've got to slow down and stay connected. We've got to do a better job of being a family."

David then opened up for the first time about his biggest fears. "The other kids are brutal," he said. "The constant teasing and bullying, the stupid cliques, the struggle to fit in—I get so sick of it all. I just want to live a normal life."

"I didn't realize that life has been so tough for you," his father responded. "But we're going to work through these troubles—together."

As I sat back and watched the generations bond, I began to see clearly how, in one family after another, (1) worry and stress are dealing heavy blows and (2) our high-octane lifestyles seem to be making things worse.

While adventure and adrenaline go hand in hand, our *homes* need to be peaceful environments, safe havens from the hectic world around us. Yet the medical doctors and psychologists I've talked to say the average American family could make Indiana Jones seem boring. It's not surprising that so many feel helpless throughout their plunges down the rapids of fear, worry, and anxiety.

Perhaps you'll discover what the guys and I saw so clearly on the river.

"STUCK IN THE CROSSCURRENTS"

That's how Jeffery described his life back in Grand Rapids, Michigan. And it took huge doses of adrenaline on Colorado's Gunnison River to help him see it.

"Everything is so upside-down in my world," he says. "I work endless hours to pay for a big mortgage and all the things that go with it: electronic toys and gadgets that end up keeping us apart even when we're under the same roof. Most of the time we're on the go, sort of stuck in the crosscurrents—constantly moving but not really connecting. And that has to change."

Even some in the mainstream media are waving a white flag. As Tim Kreider said in the op-ed section of the *New York Times*:

Busyness serves as a kind of existential reassurance, a hedge against emptiness; obviously your life cannot possibly be silly or trivial or meaningless if you are so busy, completely booked, in demand every hour of the day.… I can't help but wonder whether all this histrionic exhaustion isn't a way of covering up the fact that most of what we do doesn't matter.[1]

I think these observations are dead-on.

Our lives are moving at a frantic pace. Most of us are *busy being busy*. And here's another sad reality: Even our kids' lives often are scheduled down to the half-hour. School activities, clubs, other extracurricular commitments, sporting events, daycare, play dates…

Along the way, we're becoming more and more disconnected—from our families, from our friends, from our coworkers, even from God.

We spend countless hours supposedly plugged in: surfing, e-mailing, posting, texting, tweeting … staring at screens, typing quickly but not meaningfully interacting. We rarely talk to our neighbors, let alone know their names. Even in church we press through the crowds, slide into a pew or chair, and become spectators. We blend in … but we don't truly connect.

When we stop connecting with someone or something outside ourselves, we become anxious. When we start feeling that way, we frequently try to cope by escaping. More and more, the felt need for relief from anxiety and worry is leading us into addictions of a thousand kinds.

We're flooded with messages exhorting us toward this or that sort of "perfection"—things will be ideal if we buy this or acquire that. The values of consumerism, materialism, and instant gratification serve only to amplify the void many of us feel day after day after day.[2] Again, as our busyness escalates and we come under more stress, we're turning *from* the connections that offer help (with God and with others) and *toward* thought patterns and actions that just leave us more worried and anxious. More and more we are losing our compass.

FINALLY ... *REAL* SOLUTIONS

As a professional in the mental health field—and someone who's seen lives torn apart by the misuse of drugs, prescription and otherwise—I (Arnie) advise extreme caution and plain old common sense as we consider the role of pharmaceutical medications. They can be effective in the treatment of anxiety and stress, but remember: abuse medicine, and you're playing Russian roulette with your life.

God did not create us to be addicts. But because we live in a fallen world that has not yet been restored, and because until Christ returns or calls us home we all will battle against sin, the same psychological, neurological, and spiritual dynamics of full-fledged addiction are actively at work in every human being. In the words of Dr. Gerald G. May: "The same processes that are responsible for addiction to alcohol and narcotics are also responsible for addiction to ideas, work, relationships, power, moods, fantasies, and an endless variety of other things. We are all addicts in every sense of the word."[3]

Accordingly, viewing medication as a cure-all for worry and stress is a mistake. I believe we must do much more than relieve the symptoms of what's bugging us; we must get to the causes, addressing the problem at its source. In addition to adrenaline oversaturation, we must evaluate five key aspects of our lives:

Our Diet—Are we getting the nutrition we need?

Our Aerobic Health—Are we getting regular aerobic exercise?

Our Need for Relaxation—Are we making ample time for rest and restoration?

Our Need for Sleep—Are we getting what we need every day?

Our Overall Lifestyle—Are we pursuing a less driven, more balanced life?

Now for the flipside of this issue: While anxiety meds aren't a cure-all, they're often a *must* for those who struggle with severe anxiety—especially at the beginning of a wellness program. (So I am not necessarily replacing my medication with a cup of herbal tea—and neither should you!) Those battling panic disorder, agoraphobia, obsessive-compulsive disorder, and post-traumatic stress disorder, for example, often can benefit tremendously from the right pharmaceutical drug.

My advice: Talk with your family physician and with a licensed therapist. Get a complete physical and full mental health evaluation. To help you take that step, I've asked a couple of medical professionals to offer their perspectives on the question of anxiety meds and/or natural remedies. My intention here is not to present a debate, with one side seeking to prove the other wrong, but rather to raise awareness of multiple solutions for combating and defeating worry.

TIME TO GET OUT OF THE CANOE

What steps can we take toward change? Try the following.

Unplug

The average US household has three TVs (each with dozens of channels), three computers, two gaming systems, and multiple smart phones, tablets, and MP3 players as well as countless other devices and "connections." While life in front of the screen can distract from anxiety, it likewise can (and very often does) have the reverse effect. What's more, it's a hindrance to building deeper connections with the ones we love.

Slow Down

Instead of having the necessary resources to process things cognitively and spiritually (in a meditative way), we're constantly on the go—and we constantly feel stressed (if not also anxious and worried). This is happening because our bodies are pumping adrenaline and cortisol. The key: force yourself to step back and slow down.

Further, there's a secret to survival that's exercised by EMTs—not to mention disaster-relief workers, lifeguards, police officers, and fire-rescue personnel. Ask them, "Why did this person survive, while that person didn't?" and often they'll say: "Survivors keep their wits about them." In other words, people who can manage their adrenaline levels under stress put themselves in a better position to handle what life brings. It's something we all need to learn.

Get Some Sleep

God doesn't want us to push through the day feeling weary and worn out. The fact is, too little shut-eye can drain our brain.

"Sleep is absolutely vital to your health and well-being," explains Dr. Don Colbert. "During sleep, you actually recharge your mind and body. It allows your body to recuperate and restore itself from exhaustion."[4]

In addition, Dr. Colbert says sleep enables our cells to regenerate and rejuvenate because our bodies secrete growth hormones that repair tissues and organs. Conversely, a lack of sleep can lead to serious health consequences and jeopardize our safety and the safety of individuals around us. For example, short sleep duration is linked with:

- Increased risk of motor vehicle accidents
- Increase in body mass index—a greater likelihood of obesity due to increased appetite caused by sleep deprivation
- Increased risk of diabetes and heart problems
- Increased risk for psychiatric conditions including depression and substance abuse
- Decreased ability to pay attention, react to signals, or remember new information

Says Dr. Maiken Nedergaard, codirector of the Center for Translational Neuromedicine at the University of Rochester Medical Center:

We have a cleaning system that almost stops when we are awake and starts when we sleep. It's almost like opening and closing a faucet—it's that dramatic. The brain has different functional states when asleep and when awake. In fact, the restorative nature of sleep appears to be the result of the active clearance of the by-products of neural activity that accumulate during wakefulness.… You can think of it like having a house party. You can either entertain guests or clean up the house, but you can't really do both at the same time.[5]

᠁

Dr. Archibald Hart, a licensed psychologist and board-certified diplomat fellow in psychopharmacology, points to the solution: "You must come down from the 'hills' of stress and into the 'valleys' of rest on a daily basis." He explains that our bodies are designed not for continuous fear, worry, and anxiety but for ongoing tranquility with short bursts of adrenaline.[6]

And the apostle Paul gives us the most important solution of all:

Here's what I want you to do, God helping you: Take your everyday, ordinary life—your sleeping, eating, going-to-work, and walking-around life—and place it before God as an offering. Embracing what God does for you is the best thing you can do for him. Don't become so well-adjusted to your culture that you fit into it without

Our Research Says . . .

- We're wired to worry first and to think second. According to neuroscientist Joseph LeDoux, connections from the limbic (emotional) systems to the cortex (cognitive) systems are stronger than connections from the cognitive systems to the emotional systems.[8]

- It's possible to retrain yourself to let your mind override your limbic system. In fact, research reveals that cognitive-behavioral therapy changes the neural circuits involved in regulating worry and anxiety.

- Worry has been shown to increase and decrease heart rate. The effects are still evident up to two hours after the worrying episode.

even thinking. Instead, fix your attention on God. You'll be changed from the inside out. Readily recognize what he wants from you, and quickly respond to it. Unlike the culture around you, always dragging you down to its level of immaturity, God brings the best out of you, develops well-formed maturity in you.[7]

Recap and Reflect

Talking Points for Couples or Group Study

- Adrenaline is a major culprit for stress—and can be addicting.

  - Evaluate your lifestyle (and those of others in your care). *Would I describe my day as a triple shot of espresso, a cup of chamomile tea, or sort of a "green tea" combo of the two? Am I constantly revved up, or* (as Dr. Hart recommends) *am I able to "come down from the mountain" at some point during the day?*

- Arnie identified five key areas we must evaluate: diet, health, need for relaxation, importance of sleep, overall lifestyle. (Flip back to mid-chapter to review.)

  - Share how you've assessed these areas. *Are there changes I need to make?*

Chapter Seven

THE SECRET OF SURRENDER

*H*ome—that was Barbara's favorite place.[1] It didn't matter that her 1960s rancher wasn't anybody else's idea of a dream home … or that the carpet and paint showed some wear and tear … or that her elderly mother, three dogs, and four cats had to manage with cramped quarters … not to mention a toilet that wouldn't stop running. The place was definitely rough around the edges—*a little like me,* she thought—yet it was stout. It had heart and a solid foundation.

Most of all, it was *home.*

Before turning in for the night, ending another hectic day that bounced from working in retail to managing her "zoo" (Barbara had a weakness for stray pets), she stole a few quiet moments on her back patio. Besides, she couldn't sleep anyway, couldn't shut off her anxious mind. Nothing new. So she settled into a comfy chair and pressed a steaming mug of decaf to her lips. The strong aroma of French roast coffee beans never failed to carry away the usual smells of the horse ranch across the field: leather, hay, smoldering fire pits, musky stables.

She took a long, slow sip, and then gazed at the Idaho sky.

"Perfect," she whispered. Endless blue had given way to countless stars. Intense white lights skipped and danced around milky clusters of yellow and purple. Shooting stars raced across the horizon.

For many years, Barbara enjoyed this nightly retreat in her own backyard. It had a way of captivating her thoughts … resetting her focus … reminding her, "God is in control." The middle-aged mom thought about how our heavenly Father never leaves things as they are. He's always at work … creating, perfecting, regenerating—*reclaiming what's his.*

She took another sip and began talking aloud to her Savior: "You've given me so much, and I deserve none of it. You know my stubborn heart, my thoughts, my hang-ups—my past."

Barbara regretted so many decisions and actions from her younger years: racking up so much debt that she and her family could barely make ends meet; eventual divorce that all but crushed her daughter's heart; more overspending; putting selfish needs first; coveting; worrying. *Stupid,* she thought. *I did a bunch of stupid things. I lived in darkness, wasting precious time.*

Even after she'd prayed and committed her life to Jesus, Barbara could not let go of the past. Day after day she hobbled along spiritually as if her heart were in shackles. And for more than a decade she hid behind a mask, letting the world see a tough lady, an unbreakable wife and mother. But on the inside she was grieving—beating herself up, constantly feeling immobilized and neutralized by fear, worry, and anxiety.

Lord—so often I catch myself feeling afraid, Barbara prayed. *I know I should let go and trust you more. But in the heat of worry, I fear that you won't catch me; like maybe you'll abandon me … and*

*my problem will be unbearable. Silly—I know. But it's what I think
sometimes.*

❧

A few days later, right in the middle of her backyard, something
remarkable happened: Barbara came clean with Christ. She
found the courage to release every festering memory, to surrender every doubt … every anxious thought that swirled around
her brain.

She had just launched into a mundane chore—watering trees,
shrubs, grass … even the bare ground her dogs had trampled. As
she tugged on the hose, moving it mechanically, rhythmically …
drenching every clump and pebble … her mind began to flood
with thought after thought. Most were painful.

Child of God? Christ-follower? Liar. That's who I really am.

She took a few more steps and sprayed the yard's center.
*Fool—that's what I am. Forgiven? How can I ever be forgiven for
my idiocy? My lack of common sense?*

"Let it go."

Barbara froze in her tracks and looked around.

"Release it."

She nearly dropped the hose. God had her attention. She
sensed him compelling her heart, extending a hand that would
pull her from her emotional pit.

"Trust me."

But she was afraid to take his hand. *I can't, Lord … I just can't.
I'm the "captain of my ship, master of my destiny," as they say. I
know right from wrong, and I made all those choices. That's why
I just—*

"No, Barbara. This is wrong. I am God, and I have forgiven you. Yet you haven't forgiven yourself."

This time she dropped the hose and broke into tears.

There she stood—alone with her Creator. Water gushing everywhere, puddles rising in the mud, and tears rolling down her cheeks. And then she began to laugh and cry, all at the same time.

Yes. You are right!

She paused and considered carefully the truth that was staring her in the face. *Yes—I really haven't forgiven myself. Yet, Lord, I now see that you have. I can let go. I am free!*

Barbara felt like jumping and dancing in the mud. She wanted to scream from the bottom of her lungs.

Thank you, God! I get it now. Thank you, thank you—

Suddenly, the cross made much more sense. Salvation through Christ—her redemption—was real! Even though she'd beaten herself up day after day, her Savior had been mending all those broken pieces, taking apart the mask, releasing the shackles, and wiping away the tears.

Peace I leave with you; my peace I give to you. Not as the world gives do I give to you. Let not your hearts be troubled, neither let them be afraid.[2]

UNCERTAINTY OR SURRENDER?

Sometimes the scariest places to be are in the safety of our warm beds, especially when our minds are reeling with countless what-ifs, robbing us of needed rest and tranquility.

Twelve hundred miles away from Barbara's home in Idaho, Peg in Omaha can't shut off the catastrophic thoughts racing through her mind. After tossing and turning half the night, she heads to her bathroom. Inside the medicine cabinet is a temporary when-most-needed relief from insomnia: a ten-milligram capsule of Zaleplon that her doctor prescribed. Lately, though, the "when-most-needed" for this forty-year-old mother has become nightly ritual. "When my head hits the pillow, I simply cannot shut off my mind," she says. Fearful thoughts take over:

Will my husband weather the storms at work … and get to keep his job?

Can we get back on track with our mortgage payments?

Why is my ten-year-old getting into fights at school?

Can my dad survive his stroke—or is a fatal one imminent?

Will a move to Maine give us the fresh start we need?

Three hours south in Kansas City, Mark is dealing with an impossible situation at the office. His job description clearly says he must be at his desk by 8:45 every weekday morning. It also says he must unlock all side doors at the beginning of his shift. But his card key won't let him in until precisely 8:45. There is no physical way he can make all this happen at the exact same time. He has requested to have the access times changed so he could enter the building earlier. But these requests are handled over at corporate, which has continued to deny his request.

To Mark, this seems like such a no-brainer. Give him the tools to do his job, or change the requirements. But his boss, a real jerk, continues to give him bad reports for not accomplishing his duties on time. If he gets one more, he'll go on probation. The folks on probation are always the first to go when layoffs start. He can't afford to be out of work. He can barely pay his bills now. Living paycheck to paycheck is stressful, but it's better than not having a paycheck at all.

Mark spends his lunch breaks surfing online for job openings. *Wow—lots of jobs for nurses out there.* But he knows that even if he finds a job for which he's qualified, his boss will never give him a good recommendation. He's stuck. Stuck in an impossible job with no hope for a better future. He works hard. He goes over and beyond. Yet coworkers who goof off and just do enough to get by continue to be promoted over him.

Frustration wells up inside as he sits at his desk. *There's no way out. I am STUCK.*

※

Barbara, Peg, and Mark aren't alone. Each evening, their brains go into fight-or-flight mode, shifting from "tranquility" to "survival." Their thoughts become imbalanced, literally overloaded with stress hormones. The physiological presence of stress, in turn, causes body and mind to stress out about feeling stressed, leading to a downward spiral.

As we saw in chapters 2 and 3, the spiral's outcome is trouble sleeping, fatigue, depression, and even physical aches and pains. Each day the struggles are left untreated, their bodies weaken and their anxiety levels grow. Fear-worry-anxiety can eventually become a health killer.

But for Barbara, the anxiety stemmed from a lack of surrender to Jesus Christ: a lack of trust in his plan and provision for her. God makes clear that this kind of worry displeases him.

Watch yourselves lest your hearts be weighed down with dissipation and drunkenness and cares of this life, and that day come upon you suddenly like a trap. For it will come upon all who dwell on the face of the whole earth. But stay awake at all times, praying that you may have strength to escape all these things that are going to take place, and to stand before the Son of Man.[3]

But now, God's Message, the God who made you in the first place, Jacob, the One who got you started, Israel: "Don't be afraid, I've redeemed you. I've called your name. You're mine. When you're in over your head, I'll be there with you. When you're in rough waters, you will not go down. When you're between a rock and a hard place, it won't be a dead end—because I am God, your personal God, the Holy of Israel, your Savior. I paid a huge price for you: all of Egypt, with rich Cush and Seba thrown in! That's how much you mean to me! That's how much I love you! I'd sell off the whole world to get you back, trade the creation just for you."[4]

Do not worry about your life, what you will eat or drink; or about your body, what you will wear. Is not life more important than food, and the body more important than clothes? Look at the birds of the air; they do not sow or reap or store away in barns, and yet your heavenly Father feeds them. Are you not much more valuable than they? Can any one of you by worrying add a single hour to your life?[5]

THE KEY: BECOMING "WORRY-WISE"

Passages like these aren't suggesting that Barbara (and all of us) are condemned because we worry or that we should never be concerned about anything. Paul tells us to stop perpetually worrying about the same things—ruminating about the same things over and over. (See Philippians 4:6 and flip back to our discussion in chapter 2 for a refresher.) And he gives us the prescription for curing our worries: we're to bring our requests to God with an attitude of thanksgiving, expecting that what awaits us is God's peace, which surpasses all understanding.

The very serious spiritual problem is that our lives become filled with fear and worry when we refuse to surrender all to Jesus. When we decline to be joined to our Creator, even when he has provided us a way back to himself through Christ, we settle down into the bog of our own anxiety.[6]

We need to embrace the big picture. Every moment is only a sliver when you take time to step back and look at your life as a whole. And yet these slivers aren't insignificant at all. They're the building blocks of our lives. The small decisions we make daily build the foundation of our own big picture. If we dwell on the mistakes, then we're reinforcing them. If we decide daily to start fresh and move forward, then we're building a stronger base for our future.

Know this: positive thinking can only go so far without being challenged by reality. We must dig deeper and identify the source of our motivation. *Who am I in the sight of my Creator? Why am I here? What am I to do with my life?* The answers to these questions cannot be found on the surface of our lives. They do not begin with our job titles or accomplishments. They come from a much deeper place. It's a place that gives birth to our self-identity and worldview. And once we go deep down and wrestle with our inner selves, then we can begin to identify who we are and why we're here.

It's often a messy battle as we sift through our beliefs and our past. But as we emerge on the other side, we begin to see how the puzzle pieces fit together. As the big picture begins to take shape, we're able to find our place. And suddenly the worries found in the slivers of time seem so very small. Our focus shifts from the problems to our responses. And from this view we're able to give thanks to God for all the opportunities we have to trust him. He is just waiting for us to release our burdens and worries into his care.

READING TO START LIVING WORRY-FREE?

Did you see your face among any of the sufferers you met in this book?

Take comfort in being reminded that you're not alone. While only a medical professional can accurately diagnose your condition (and the conditions of loved ones in your care), there are steps we all can take, including lifestyle changes, to calm down and worry less. (Go back and review our Worry-Wise Plan in chapters 3 through 5 as often as necessary.)

But before we end our conversation, let's check back in with Barbara to see the progress she has made. Finally learning to surrender control really *is* paying off.

Even now as a mature believer, Barbara knows she still doesn't have it all together. Just when she thinks she has finally mastered this whole fear-worry-stress cycle, another anxious thought pops into her mind. Before she knows it, she is fretting again. First it is an excessive preoccupation with life's uncertainties. Then it's constant "what-if" thoughts that seem to stab at her stomach. Then it's panic—even anger.

Is this just how it is in life—all the way to the end?

She still loves to sit in her backyard retreat. This time she takes a deep breath and pictures the faces of her family today—from the perfect smile of her beautiful daughter (now married, with kids of her own) to her sweet ninety-two-year-old mother, still in her care. Even her "zoo" of scruffy pets soothes her heart. *Lord, thank you for my home—my little bit of heaven on earth. Thank you for your grace. You forgive … and then give, and give, and give. Help me to trust more … to change what needs to be changed. Amen.*

Barbara knows that tomorrow will bring a new batch of challenges. "In this world we will have tribulation," she reminds herself.

But this time, Barbara is ready.

You will be ready too.

Our Research Says …

▸ Our survey respondents rated seeking God's love and care, reading or listening to Scripture, and looking for a stronger connection with God as "most helpful" for coping with worry.

▸ Adults and teens who engage Scripture most days of the week are more comfortable with uncertainty, are able to trust God more, and worry less than those who do not.

Recap and Reflect

Talking Points for Couples or Group Study

1. Consider this observation from C. S. Lewis:

The almost impossible thing is to hand over your whole self—all your wishes and precautions—to Christ. But it is far easier than what you are trying to do instead. For what we are trying to do is remain what we call "ourselves," to keep personal happiness as our great aim in life, and yet at the same time be "good." We are all trying to let our mind and heart go their own way—centered on money or pleasure or ambition—and hoping, in spite of this, to behave honestly and chastely and humbly. And that is exactly what Christ warned us you could not do.[7]

> ❋ *Am I able to give up control and surrender my will to God's will? If not, what's keeping me from doing so? If so, in what practical ways will this bring relief from worry?*

2. Read Romans 8:38–39:

I am convinced that neither death nor life, neither angels nor demons, neither the present nor the future, nor any powers, neither height nor depth, nor anything else in all creation, will be able to separate us from the love of God that is in Christ Jesus our Lord.

> ❋ *Do I believe this? In what ways can this truth free me from worry?*

ENDNOTES

Starting Point: When Worry Hits Home

1 American Psychological Association, "Stressed in America," apa.org, January 2011, apa.org/monitor/2011/01/stressed-america.aspx.

2 Melissa Dahl, "Millennials are the most stressed-out generation, new survey finds," nbcnews.com, accessed February 8, 2013, vitals.nbcnews.com/_news/2013/02/07/16889472-millennials-are-the-most-stressed-out-generation-new-survey-finds?lite.

3 Dr. Mona Spiegel, "Anxiety on the Rise," selfgrowth.com, accessed February 11, 2013, selfgrowth.com/articles/anxiety_on_the_rise.

4 John 10:10.

5 Matthew 6:33–34 (on "all these things," see vv. 26–32).

6 T. D. Borkovec, E. Robinson, T. Pruzinsky, and J. A. DePree, "Preliminary Exploration of Worry: Some Characteristics and Processes," *Behaviour Research and Therapy*, vol. 21, no. 1 (1983), 9–16.

7 Hans Selye, "A Syndrome Produced by Diverse Nocuous Agents," *Nature* (1936).

8 T. H. Holmes and R. H. Rahe, "The Social Readjustment Rating Scale," *Journal of Psychosomatic Research*, vol. 11, no. 2 (1967), 213–18.

Chapter 1: Secret of Wisdom

1 American Psychological Association, "Stress in America Findings," apa.org, 2010, http://www.apa.org/news/press/releases/stress/2010/national-report.pdf.

2 Joshua 1:6–9 ESV.

3 Rosmarin, D. H., S. Pirutinsky, R. P. Auerbach, T. Björgvinsson, J. Bigda-Peyton, G. Andersson, K. I. Pargament, and E. J. Krumrei, "Incorporating

spiritual beliefs into a cognitive model of worry," *Journal of Clinical Psychology*, vol. 67 (2011), 1–10.

4   Adrian Wells, *Metacognitive Therapy for Anxiety and Depression* (New York: Guilford, 2008).

5   Again, those born between 1979 and 1995.

Chapter Two: The Secret of Self-Awareness

1   Martin M. Antony and Peter J. Norton, *The Anti-Anxiety Workbook* (New York: Guilford, 2008), 26.

2   Ibid.

3   For a thorough discussion, read chapter 2, "The GABA-Anxiety Connection," in Dr. Archibald D. Hart's book, *The Anxiety Cure* (Nashville: Thomas Nelson, 1999).

4   Eric T. Scalise, PhD, LPC, LMFT, interview with Michael Ross, August 1, 2013.

5   Dr. Archibald D. Hart, *The Anxiety Cure* (Nashville: Thomas Nelson, 1999), 28.

6   Matthew 6:25–27 NLT.

7   Interview with Michael Ross, September 25, 2013.

8   Interview with Michael Ross, July 23, 2013.

9   National Institute of Mental Health. *What is Panic Disorder?* http://www.nimh.nih.gov/health/topics/panic-disorder/index.shtml.

Chapter 3: The Secret of Right Thinking (Calming Our Mind)

1   Richard C. Halverson, *No Greater Power* (Colorado Springs: Multnomah, 1986), 186.

2   John 14:6.

3   Mehmet Oz, MD, "Dr. Oz's Worry Cure and Diet Plan," doctoroz.com, March 12, 2012, doctoroz.com/videos/dr-ozs-worry-cure-diet-plan?.

4   Elouise Renich Fraser, *Confessions of a Beginning Theologian* (Downers Grove, IL: InterVarsity, 1998), 31.

5   Oz, "Dr. Oz's Worry Cure and Diet Plan."

6   Interview with Michael Ross, August 28, 2013.

7   See Psalm 46:10.

8   Daniel G. Amen, *Change Your Brain, Change Your Life* (New York: Three Rivers, 1998), 59–60.

9   Psalm 46:10.

10 John Sachem, "Inspirational Stress Relief Quotes," Yahoo! Voices, April 29, 2010, http://voices.yahoo.com/inspirational-stress-relief-quotes-5933076.html.

Chapter 4: The Secret of Healthy Living (De-Stressing Our Body)

1   Bob Anderson, *Stretching: 30th Anniversary Edition* (Bolinas, CA: Shelter, 2010), 9.

2   Sara Reistad-Long, "How to Combat Every Kind of Stress," *Women's Day*, February 11, 2013, http://www.womansday.com/health-fitness/wellness /advice/a1355/how-to-combat-every-kind-of-stress-103847/.

3   "Stress: The Silent Killer," Holisticonline.com, holisticonline.com/stress /stress_diet.htm.

4   Mayo Clinic Staff, "Sodium: How to Tame Your Salt Habit," mayoclinic.org, mayoclinic.com/health/sodium/NU00284.

5   Joseph McAllister, "What Do Salt & Sugar Do to Your Body?" Livestrong. com, June, 3, 2011, livestrong.com/article/461835-what-do-salt-sugar-do-to-your-body/.

6   Reginald B. Cherry, MD, *Dr. Cherry's Little Instruction Book: Health and Healing* (Minneapolis: Bethany House, 2003), 138.

7   David Zinczenko with Matt Goulding, *Eat This, Not That: All New Supermarket Survival Guide* (New York: Rodale, 2012), 117.

8   Lawrence Robinson, Maya W. Paul, MA, and Jeanne Segal, PhD, "Healthy Eating: Easy Tips for Planning a Healthy Diet and Sticking to It," helpguide .org, last updated March 2015, helpguide.org/life/healthy_eating_diet.htm.

9   "Nutrition and Food, Well-Done, Men's Health, Eat like a (healthy) Man. Men's Health can help." Editors of Men's Health, Men'sHealth.com, July 23, 2014, http://www.menshealth.com/nutrition/nutrition-food-well-done?cm_mmc=Facebook-_-MensHealth-_-Content-Nutrition-_-SugareyFood.

Chapter 5: The Secret of Christ-Centered Growth (Transforming Our Spirit)

1 Doug Banister, *Sacred Quest* (Grand Rapids: Zondervan, 2001), 14–15.

2 Ibid.

3 Dr. Henry Cloud, *Changes That Heal* (Grand Rapids: Zondervan, 1992), 49.

4 R. C. Sproul, *Effective Prayer* (Wheaton, IL: Tyndale, 1984), 32.

5 See Philippians 4:6; 1 Timothy 2:1–3.

6 See 2 Chronicles 7:14.

7 Mark 11:22–23.

8 Margaret Magdalen, *Jesus, Man of Prayer* (Downers Grove, IL: InterVarsity, 1987), 51.

9 Mary Fairchild, "How Do Christians Deal with Stress?" About.com Christianity, http://christianity.about.com/od/faqhelpdesk/f/dealwithstress.htm.

10 Psalm 91:3–6 CEV.

11 Philippians 4:6–7 NKJV.

12 Colossians 3:15, MSG.

13 Fairchild, "How Do Christians Deal with Stress?"

14 James 4:8.

15 Henry T. Blackaby and Richard Blackaby, *Experiencing God Day-By-Day Devotional* (Nashville: Broadman & Holman, 1998), 360.

16 John 14:1 NRSV.

17 John 14:15–17 NRSV.

18 John 16:13 NRSV.

19 In Dorothy M. Stewart, *The Westminster Collection of Christian Prayers* (Louisville: Westminster John Knox, 2002), 9.

20 Ibid, 10.

21 Ibid, 278.

22 Max Lucado, "30 Days of Thoughts (From Great Day Every Day)," maxlucado.com, March 22, 2007, http://maxlucado.com/read/topical/30-days-of-thoughts-from-every-day-deserves-a-chance/.

23 See James 4:8.

24 1 John 4:18.

25 See Psalm 25:3–6.

26 Corrie ten Boom, Brainy Quote, accessed October 9, 1012, http://www
   .brainyquote.com/quotes/quotes/c/corrietenb135203.html.

27 See John 15:12–13.

28 See a longer sample list at anxietycentre.com/anxiety-famous-people.shtml.

29 Romans 12:2 NLT.

Chapter 6: The Secret of Balance

1 Tim Kreider, "The 'Busy' Trap," *New York Times*, June 30, 2012, opinionator.
   blogs.nytimes.com/2012/06/30/the-busy-trap/?_r=0.

2 Edmund J. Bourne, PhD, *Coping with Anxiety* (Oakland, CA: New
   Harbinger, 2003), 8–9.

3 Gerald G. May, MD, *Addiction and Grace* (San Francisco: Harper Collins,
   1988), 3–4.

4 Don Colbert, MD, *The New Bible Cure for Sleep Disorders* (Lake Mary, FL.:
   Siloam, 2009), 1.

5 Barbara Mantel, "A Good Night's Sleep Scrubs Your Brain Clean,
   Researchers Find," Daily Health Headlines, October 17, 2013, http://
   dailyhealthheadlines.com/article/health-headlines/a-good-nights-sleep
   -scrubs-your-brain-clean-researchers-find.

6 "The Anxiety Cure According to Dr. Archibald Hart," compiled by
   Audrey Wagner, Student Wellness Center, January 22, 2007, http://
   georgetowncollege.edu/studentwellness/2007/01/the-anxiety-cure
   -according-to-dr-archibald-hart/.

7 Romans 12:1–2 MSG.

8 Susan Krauss Whitbourne, PhD, "Turn Down Your Brain's Worry Center,"
   Psychology Today, October 9, 2012, http://www.psychologytoday.com/blog
   /fulfillment-any-age/201210/turn-down-your-brain-s-worry-center.

Chapter 7: The Secret of Surrender

1 "Barbara" is a real person, but to keep her anonymous I have altered details
   in this account of her story.

2 John 14:27 ESV.

3 Luke 21:34–36 ESV.

4 Isaiah 43:1–4 MSG.

5 Matthew 6:25–27.

6 Hart, *The Anxiety Cure*, 25.

7 C. S. Lewis, "Giving All to Christ," *Devotional Classics* eds. Richard J. Foster and James Bryan Smith (New York: HarperCollins, 1990), 9.

ACKNOWLEDGMENTS

We are deeply grateful to several psychology, medical, and ministry professionals who helped us shape these pages. Here are six we'd like to highlight:

Pamela Ovwigho, Ph.D.—executive director of the Center for Bible Engagement. She directed all of the research that became the foundation of this book and contributed to "Starting Point," as well as chapters 1 and 2.

Dr. Trina Young Greer—licensed clinical psychologist, is the founder and executive director of Genesis Counseling Center (www.genesiscounselingcenter.com) and co-founder of Genesis Assist (www.genesisassist.com).

Nanette Gingery Lankas, M.A.—therapist and addiction specialist, is the president of Summit Care and Wellness Treatment and Counseling (www.summitcareandwellness.com).

Eric T. Scalise, Ph.D., LPC, LMFT—is the vice president for professional development, executive director, international board of Christian care, and senior editor of American Association of Christian Counselor (www.aacc.net). In addition, he is the vice president for academic affairs at Light University online, as well as an author, a national and international conference speaker, and a consultant with organizations, clinicians, ministry leaders, and churches on a variety of issues.

ABOUT THE AUTHORS

Arnie Cole (EdD, Pepperdine) is the CEO of Back to the Bible and Director of Research and Development for the Center for Bible Engagement. He has spent much of his professional life tracking trends of human behavior and developing programs that can help change negative behaviors. He and his wife, Char, are the parents of adult children and operate Still Waters Ranch, an equestrian center that serves as a community outreach. The Coles live near Lincoln, Nebraska.

Michael Ross is an award-winning journalist and the author, co-author, and collaborator of more than 34 books for Christian families, including the Gold Medallion winner *BOOM: A Guy's Guide to Growing Up* (Tyndale), and a bestselling parenting guide *What Your Son Isn't Telling You* (Bethany House). Michael is the former editor of *Breakaway,* a national magazine for teen guys published by Focus on the Family. Today, he oversees Back to the Bible's book publishing efforts. He and his wife Tiffany live in Lincoln, Nebraska, with their son Christopher.

Back to the Bible is a 75-year-old radio ministry aggressively adapting to the digital age. Download the ministry's free goTandem Bible app. You can find it on Google Play, the iTunes App Store, or on www.goTandem.com.

NOTES

NOTES

NOTES

NOTES

NOTES